THE MACHINE LANGUAGE BOOK FOR THE COMMODORE 64

By: Lothar Englisch

Abacus Software
P.O. BOX 7211 GRAND RAPIDS, MICH. 49510

Second Printing, October 1984
Printed in U.S.A. Translated by Greg Dykema

ISBN 0-916439-02-X

P R E F A C E

Programming in machine and assembly language is one of those things that everyone would like to be able to do. Machine language is extremely fast and versatile. Many people try to learn it, but most quickly give it up because it is too complicated. Only a few actually use it.

With this book we want to make it possible for thousands of Commodore 64 users to use machine language. We have enlisted the services of Lothar Englisch as author for this purpose. Not only has he worked on many of our other books, but he is also well acquainted with the Commodore operating systems and programming for all models of the Commodore computers in both machine language and assembler.

To get the most out of machine language programming, you must concentrate on the following chapters. We think that you will be rewarded in the end.

Have fun with this book and much success with your own machine language programs.

Table of Contents

1. INTRODUCTION

Why use machine language? -- Advantages and disadvantages of programming in machine language

Today, when you purchase a home or personal computer such as the Commodore 64, you have the BASIC programming language available as soon as you turn your computer on. With BASIC you can perform almost all of the tasks needed in home computing. It is easy to learn to program in BASIC. Why then, should you bother with machine language? Isn't it just a relic from the Dark Ages of computing?

Let's compare BASIC to machine language.

Most of us have mastered BASIC and know that it's not very difficult to learn. In this book we'll try to convince you that programming in machine language is almost as easy to learn. If you already know BASIC, then you have a headstart. The fundamentals of programming in machine language are not much different.

What advantages over BASIC justify that you learn a new programming language?

Your Commodore 64 comes with the BASIC programming language built-in. BASIC is an acronym for Beginner's All Purpose

Symbolic Instruction Code and despite its ease of mastery, it is quite capable of performing most home computing tasks. BASIC is a high level programming languages like FORTRAN, Pascal, and COBOL. These languages are often called problem-oriented languages because they are intended to be used for solving problems in various fields such as mathematics, science or business. The counterpart of problem-oriented languages are the machine-oriented languages such as FORTH, and require a more detailed knowledge of the computer hardware. Machine language is the extreme member of this category of languages.

By itself, the Commodore 64 cannot understand BASIC at all. How can it execute the BASIC commands that you type in at the keyboard if it doesn't speak BASIC? The Commodore 64 contains an "operating system" which includes a BASIC interpreter. This interpreter converses with you in BASIC. The Commodore 64 converts the BASIC commands and statements into a series of executable machine language instructions. You don't even see this happening. It takes place "automatically".

Let's take a look at a simple example of how the BASIC interpreter works:

```
PRINT "HELLO"
```

When you enter this statement and press <RETURN>, the interpreter reads the line character by character.

One of the jobs of the interpreter is to recognize the commands (also called keywords) that make up the BASIC language. When it finds the first word in the line (PRINT), the interpreter looks in its **command table** to determine if the word is a BASIC keyword. The command table contains all of the BASIC keywords: GOTO, FOR, INPUT, PRINT, etc. Associated with each BASIC keyword is the location of the routine in the Commodore 64 operating system which performs the actions required by that BASIC keyword. Below is a simplified example of the command table:

BASIC KEYWORD	MEMORY LOCATION WHICH PERFORMS REQUIRED ACTIONS
GOTO	43168
IF	43304
INPUT	43967
.	.
.	.
PRINT	43680
.	.

If the interpreter finds the keyword in the command table, it knows what part of the operating system is to carry out that BASIC command. In our example, the interpreter searches the command table for the word **PRINT.** It finds the keyword and notes that the memory location which performs the PRINT statement begins at location 43680. Therefore, the interpreter lets the "program" segment (usually called a **routine** or machine-language routine) located at 43680 perform the PRINT command.

The **routine** at 43680 continues to read more of that same line - also character by character. Next it finds a quotation mark which tells PRINT routine that text follows. According the the rules of BASIC, the Commodore 64 echos onto the screen each of the next characters up to the ending quotation mark. So the word **HELLO** appears on the screen. If no additional characters appear on the line following the ending quotation mark, the routine knows that its job is complete and responds with **READY.** The BASIC interpreter is now ready for another command.

This may appear very complicated and you may be telling yourself that there must be an easier way. But this is exactly the purpose of the BASIC interpreter -- to insulate you from the drudgery and hard work of machine language. Why then learn machine language?

Machine language is considerably faster than BASIC.

What speed advantages does machine language have over BASIC and what accounts for this advantage? In order for your computer understand BASIC, is has a BASIC interpreter which recognizes and executes individual BASIC commands. The interpreter itself is written in machine language.

To perform a simple BASIC command, the interpreter must do several things. A simple BASIC statement is POKE 1024,10.

The interpreter searches for the first word in the statement; it finds the keyword POKE in its command table; it knows to expect two arguments; it finds the first argument 1024 and converts it to binary (remember that the computer works in binary); it finds the second argument 10 and converts it to binary; it writes this second value into the location specified by the first argument. This statement takes about two milliseconds or 2 thousandths of a second to perform.

How can you do the same task in machine language? You can peform the same thing with two instructions:

```
LDA #10
STA 1024
```

These two instructions take six microseconds or 6 millionths of a second. This is less than 1/300th the time as BASIC.

A machine language program is from 10 to 1000 times faster than an equivalent program written in BASIC.

Some tasks such as sorting or calculating mathematical formula are very time-consuming. If there are large amount of data, these tasks may easily take hours to complete using the BASIC language. Substituting a fast machine language program would be welcome in such a situation.

Some tasks cannot be performed using BASIC. An example is attending to the "interrupts" that temporarily require the Commodore 64 to stop what it's doing to see if the RUN/STOP key is pressed. Servicing interrupts must be done by a machine language routine.

This means that you cannot utilize the full capabilities of the Commodore 64 without machine language. This is especially true for high resolution graphics and the music synthesizer on the Commodore 64.

Another important point about machine language programming is its use of memory. A well-written machine language program may be ten times smaller than an equivalent BASIC program. A 1K program written in BASIC is not very large; but a 1K program written in machine language is large.

The same holds true for data storage. You can create and maintain compact data structures in machine language that are not possible in BASIC. For example, BASIC requires two bytes to represent integer values between 0 and 255. In machine language, you can represent integer values between 0 and 255 in one byte for each variable. Thus one-half of the storage space for such values is wasted using BASIC. Machine language lets you choose the most optimal data structure for each problem.

To be fair, there are disadvantages to using machine

language. First, you must learn how to program in machine language. If you have already mastered BASIC, then you have the fundamentals under your belt. But you also need some tools that let you easily write and work with machine language programs. This book contains the listings for several such tools.

Another disadvantage of machine language is that these programs can run only on the model computers for which they are written, and require substantial changes to run on a different model. Most BASIC programs are more easily transportable to other computers.

Testing machine language programs is another difficulty unless you have the appropriate tools. We have included the listing for a 6510 simulator program that not only teaches you the machine language instructions but helps you find errors in your programs.

Although machine language programming has some drawbacks, many tasks cannot be solved without machine language and many others require you to get the last bit of performance from your computer.

After you have written your first machine language program, you'll see that it isn't so difficult. We hope that you find the lessons of this book helpful and that they inspire you to solve your own computing problems in machine language.

2. The 6510 Microprocessor

Before you begin programming in machine language, you need to become acquainted with the processor itself. Let's clarify some terms first. We'll begin with the construction of the processor.

The 6510 microprocessor belongs to the family of 65XX processors that are found in most Commodore computers. The 6510 processor contains a set of registers which are used by all operations.

How can we describe the registers?

A microprocessor works digitally. It can only distinguish between two conditions. We can think of these two conditions like a switch which can be either on and off (or 1 and 0). A single switch can have only two states. By itself a switch is not very useful, so multiple switches are combined into registers.

A single switch in the processor is called a **bit** (from binary digit). A group of eight bits is called a byte. The registers of the 6510 processor contains a group of eight bits (or one byte) is arranged like this:

```
bit number    7 6 5 4 3 2 1 0    (power of 2)
contents      0 1 1 0 1 0 0 1
```

FIG 2.1

The upper row illustrates the bit numbering convention that is commonly used throughout this book. The bits are numbered from zero to seven. Beneath each bit number are the contents of the bits; either a 0 or a 1. While a bit can represent two conditions (and therefore only two values), you can represent a larger range with 8 bits.

Here's the numbering system that you are most familiar with - the decimal system.

```
decimal position     3 2 1 0     (power of 10)
    contents         5 7 2 4
```

FIG 2.2

These positions are also numbered, this time from zero to three.

How do you calculate the value of this number?
Each digit has a value between zero and nine and the next position has a value ten times greater. Starting from the rightmost decimal position:

$$4*10^0 + 2*10^1 + 7*10^2 + 5*10^3$$

$$= 4 + 2*10 + 7*10*10 + 5*10*10*10$$

$$= 4 + 2*10 + 7*100 + 5*1000$$

$$= 4 + 20 + 700 + 5000$$

$$= 5724$$

Likewise, you can determine the contents of the registers using the binary number system. They are called binary numbers because each position allows two values instead of ten. Accordingly, the next highest position is not ten times greater, but only twice the previous value. So you can calculate the contents of the register:

$$1*2^0 + 0*2^1 + 0*2^2 + 1*2^3 + 0*2^4 + 1*2^5 + 1*2^6 + 0*2^7$$
$$= 1*1 + 0*2 + 0*4 + 1*8 + 0*16 + 1*32 + 1*64 + 0*128$$
$$= 1 + 0 + 0 + 8 + 0 + 32 + 64 + 0$$
$$= 105$$

Thus the contents of the register in FIG 2.1 is 105. These troublesome calculations can be simplified, if you first calculate the value of each bit position. This is analagous to memorizing the decimal positions.

A 1 in this bit position	Is equivalent to this decimal value
0	$2^0 = 1$
1	$2^1 = 2$
2	$2^2 = 4$
3	$2^3 = 8$
4	$2^4 = 16$
5	$2^5 = 32$
6	$2^6 = 64$
7	$2^7 = 128$

What is the maximum value of the register? If all of the bit positions of the register have the value one, their sum yields 1 + 2 + 4 + 8 + 16 + 32 + 64 + 128 = 255. The greatest value that can be represented in eight bits is 255. So a total of 256 (0 thru 255) different values can be represented in a register.

But binary numbers are tedious to manipulate. For this reason, an alternative representation is introduced. It requires fewer digits and is therefore more convenient to use. If you divide an 8-bit binary number into two 4-bit binary numbers, each 4-bit number can represent 16 different values. If you construct a number system with 16 different digits, then you can express each 8-bit binary number with just two digits.

bit position	7 6 5 4	3 2 1 0
binary contents	0 1 1 0	1 0 0 1
hexadecimal contents	6	9

FIG 2.3

The hexadecimal (base 16) numbering system uses 16 different digits for this purpose. Each byte is divided into two half-bytes, called nybbles. A nybble can have values from 0 to 15, but the decimal number system only has digits from 0 to 9. In the hexadecimal number system, the digits from 10 thru 15 are represented by the letters A thru F. The hexadecimal digits are arranged like this:

This Binary Nybble	Is equivalent to this Hex digit	And has this decimal value
0000	0	0
0001	1	1
0010	2	2
0011	3	3
0100	4	4
0101	5	5
0110	6	6
0111	7	7
1000	8	8
1001	9	9
1010	A	10
1011	B	11
1100	C	12
1101	D	13
1110	E	14
1111	F	15

For the example in FIG 2.3, the contents of the register have a hexadecimal value 69. In order to distinguish between the various number systems, you denote a hexadecimal number with a preceding dollar sign **$**, and a binary number with a preceding percent sign **%**.

Appendix C is a Decimal, Hexadecimal, Binary conversion table. The remainder of this book uses hexadecimal numbers most often, since it is easily representable and convertable into the binary representation of the processor.

Now let's take a look at the microprocessor registers.

The 6510 has a total of six registers, five are eight-bit registers and the sixth is a sixteen-bit register. Let's examine the registers individually.

The **accumulator** is the most important register in the microprocessor. It is the universal working register, used for almost all operations. All arithmetic and logical operations, and almost all of the comparison instructions use the accumulator.

The **X-register** is the second register in the processor. This register is used together with the accumulator when working with tables. It functions as the counter or pointer to the individual table elements. For this reason this register is also called an index register.

The **Y-register** is an index register like the X-register and serves similar purposes.

The **program counter** is a 16-bit register. Its contents indicate the memory location from which the next instruction is to be executed. This register is managed by the microprocessor itself. Normally, you do not have direct control over the contents of this register.

The **stack pointer** points to an area of memory called the stack which is used for subroutines and for short-term data storage. The stack is described in detail later.

The **processor status register** gives information about the result of the last executed instruction. This register is the foundation for the decision making and conditional branching instructions. Seven of the eight bits of the status register are used as **flags.** You can examine and conditionally branch depending on the setting of a particular flag. A flag can be either **set** (=1) or **clear** (=0). The processor status register is made of the following flags:

bit position	7 6 5 4 3 2 1 0
flag type	N V - B D I Z C

The letters are abbreviations for the names of the flags, and have the following meanings:

C - Carry The carry flag contains the carry generated by an addition, and is set if the result is greater than 255 and therefore cannot be contained in eight bits of the accumulator.

Z - Zero The zero flag is set if the result of an operation is zero.

I - Interrupt Disable This flag determines if interrupts are permitted in a program. This flag does not interest us at the moment.

D - Decimal The decimal flag determines if arithmetic is carried out in the decimal mode.

B - Break The break flag indicates if execution was halted by a BRK instruction.

V - oVerflow The V flag indicates overflow when calculating with signed numbers.

N - Negative This flag is set if the result of an operation results in a value greater than 127 (bit 7 is set). The designation negative comes from the fact that values over $7F can be interpreted as negative numbers.

A microprocessor must have a place to get data and store data. The computer's memory serves this purpose. Memory is divided into individual cells containing 8 bits each, the same size as the accumulator and X and Y registers. In order to access the memory, it must be possible to select a specific memory location. This selection is called **addressing** memory. We give each memory location a number or **address.** With 8 bits, the microprocessor can address cells from 0 to 255 for a total of 256 memory cells. This is far too few for most applications. For this reason, the microprocessor uses 16-bits for the address. With 16 bits, the microprocessor can address 2^{16} = 65536 memory locations.

This is called a 16-bit address bus. To summarize - a) the 6510 microprocessor can address 65536 memory locations; b) each memory location can contain a value from 0 to 255. For ease of handling, 2^{10} = 1024 bytes is called a kilobyte or 1K. Therefore, the processor can address 64*1024 = 65536 or 64K. This is the entire address range of the Commodore 64.

Now you can understand the significance of the program counter. The program counter contains a 16-bit value. This 16-bit value is the address of the next instruction that the microprocessor is to fetch from memory and execute.

An instruction for the microprocessor can be represented by a value between 0 and 255. The 6510 microprocessor can have a maximum of 256 different instructions. However, not all the codes have a meaning on the 6510; fewer than 256 instructions exist. BASIC commands are naturally not included.

3. Instructions and Addressing Modes of the 6510

Of the 256 possible 8-bit codes, 151 are legal instructions for the 6510. These include several similar instructions, that are different only by **addressing mode.** There are only 56 entirely different instructions on the 6510. These instructions are easy to learn. They are introduced to you in groups.

An instruction is represented in the computer as an 8-bit binary number. Each particular machine language instruction has a specific binary value. The microprocessor knows what actions to take based on this binary value.

Machine language instructions are given **mnemonic** names. A mnemonic is a three character abbreviation for a machine language operation. For example, the mnemonic **LDA** stands for **L**oa**D** **A**ccumulator. These mnemonics will become more familiar to you as we discuss them throughout the book.

Now let's take a look at the specific instructions:

A. The LOAD instructions

The LOAD instructions get data from memory and place it into a register. There are three working registers in the processor (the accumulator, the X-register and the Y-register). Each has a corresponding load instructions.

```
LDA   LoaD Accumulator
LDX   LoaD X register
LDY   LoaD Y register
```

The 6510 processor has different addressing modes. An addressing mode tells the 6510 how to calculate the address (or location) of the operand.

In the examples that follow, we show you corresponding "pseudo-BASIC" statements to illustrate the machine langauge instructions in a familiar notation.

1) Immediate Addressing

```
LDA #10
```

This addressing mode is indicated by the pound sign # preceding the value to be loaded. Immediate addressing means that the accumulator is loaded with the value which follows it, in this case 10. The corresponding pseudo-BASIC instruction is:

```
A=10
```

This addressing mode is used to load a register with a constant. It also works with the X and Y registers:

```
LDX #$7F     or     LDY #0
```

Here the X-register is loaded with the value $7F (127 in decimal) and the Y-register with the value zero (0).

When using the immediate addressing mode, the value to be loaded is part of the program. The instruction and the value are placed one after the other in two adjacent memory locations. For example, if the machine language program is located at address 1200, the program counter contains the value 1200. The 6510 microprocessor gets the intruction at 1200 and sees that its value is $A9 or decimal 169. It knows that the instruction is LDA #. So it places the contents contained in the next memory location 1201 into the accumulator (see diagram which follows). Since this instruction consists of two bytes - the instruction itself and the value to be loaded - the processor automatically increments the program counter by two. The program counter then points to the next instruction to be executed by the microprocessor starting at 1202.

```
                -------------
                !      !      !
  contents-->   !  A9  !data  !
                !      !      !
                -------------
  address--->  1200   1201   1202
```

2) Absolute Addressing

This addressing mode is used if a register is be loaded with the contents of a particular memory location. This is different from the immediate addressing mode which loads the register with a constant value.

```
    LDA $C0AF
```

Here the accumulator is loaded with the contents of memory location $C0AF. How is this instruction represented in memory? The address $C0AF is a 16-bit number. A memory location can only hold 8 bits. The solution is to divide the 16-bit address into two 8-bit numbers. The following convention is used for this - immediately following the instruction is the least significant part of the address (low-byte) and followed by the the most significant part (high-byte).

```
                -------------------
                !      !      !      !
  contents-->   ! AD   ! AF   ! C0   !
                !      !      !      !
                -------------------
  address--->  1200   1201   1202   1203
```

In this example, the instruction code is $AD (173). The absolute address follows: with the low-byte first, $AF (175) and finally the high-byte $C0 (192). After the instruction is executed, the program counter is incremented by three. The corresponding instruction in pseudo-BASIC is:

```
A = PEEK($C0AF)
```

This instruction also works with the X and Y registers. The instruction or operation codes, abbreviated to **op codes**, can be found in Appendix A.

When executing absolute addressing mode instructions, the processor gets the low-byte and then the high-byte of the address. The data found at that address is placed into the accumulator, the program counter is incremented by three and the next instruction is fetched. These instructions require three bytes, in contrast to the immediate addressing mode which requires only two.

Now a quick look at the status register. Load instructions affect the zero and negative flags. If the value loaded has a value of zero, then the zero flag is set; otherwise it is cleared. If the value loaded is negative (greater than $7F or 127 decimal), then the negative flag is set; otherwise it is cleared.

3) Zero-page addressing

Another addressing mode is called the zero-page addressing mode. This addressing mode can be used if the address of the data is in memory locations between 0 and $FF (255). This results in a two-byte instruction in contrast to the three-byte instruction of the absolute addressing mode. Zero-page addressing instructions occupy less memory and execute faster. A disadvantage, of course, is that the data must be located in addresses from 0 to 255.

Where did the term zero-page originate? You can think of the 64K of memory as being divided into 256 **pages**, each containing 256 bytes. Thus memory locations 0 thru 255 form page zero.

A zero-page load instruction looks like this:

```
LDA $73
```

```
                 -------------
                 !     !     !
contents-->      ! A5  ! 73  !
                 !     !     !
                 -------------
address--->     1200  1201  1202
```

It is stored as a two-byte instruction: $A5 (165) $73 (115). In pseudo-BASIC, this is:

```
A = PEEK($73)
```

4) Indexed Addressing

Another addressing mode is the indexed addressing mode. Here the X and Y registers play important roles.

```
LDA $25B8,X
```

This is called absolute addressing indexed by X. How does it work? The processor loads the accumulator not with the contents of memory location $25B8. Rather it first adds the value of the X-register to the absolute address ($25B8). If the X-register contains $35, for example, the following calculation takes place:

```
$25B8 + $35 = $25ED
```

The accumulator is loaded with the contents of location $25ED. If this instruction is executed with varying X-values, a different value is loaded each time. This addressing mode is very useful for programming loops and when working with tables. Other examples are described later. In pseudo-BASIC, this addressing mode can be formulated as follows:

```
A = PEEK($25B8 + X)
```

Here X implies the contents of the X register.

```
                  -------------------
                  !     !     !     !
contents-->       ! BD  ! B8  ! 25  !
                  !     !     !     !
                  -------------------
address--->     1200  1201  1202  1203
```

You can also use the Y-register in place of the X-register for indexed addressing.

```
LDA $25B8,Y
```

Here the contents of the Y-register is added to the absolute address $25B8 to obtain the final address. Using both registers, you have two independent index variables which can be used for programming nested loops.

5) Zero-page indexed addressing

Indexed addressing can also be used together with zero-page addressing, thereby carrying over the advantages of zero-page addressing to indexed addressing. Note that this addressing mode works with the X-register only. A typical instruction might look like this:

```
LDA $BA,X
```

This results in a two-byte instruction.

```
                 -------------
                 !     !     !
contents-->      ! B5  ! BA  !
                 !     !     !
                 -------------
address--->     1200  1201  1202
```

6) Indirect Indexed Addressing

This addressing mode is not as easy to understand, but permits very flexible programming -the indirect indexed addressing mode. Using this addressing mode, zero page plays an important role. With indirect indexed addressing, two consecutive memory locations in zero-page form a pointer to the actual address. The first memory cell contains the low-byte and the next contains the high-byte of the actual address. An example clarifies this.

Imagine that zero-page address $70 contains the value $20, and address $71 contains the value $C8. These two memory locations form a pointer to the address $C820. Next the Y-register also comes into play in the indexing. If the Y-register contains $B3 for example, it is added to $C820 to get an effective address of $C8D3 as shown below:

```
LDA ($70),Y   ($70)  =>    $20     contents of $70
              ($71)  =>    $C8     contents of $71
                         $C820   yields this address
              (Y)    =>    $B3     contents of Y reg.
                         $C8D3   sum of addr and Y reg.
           ($C8D3)   =>    $4F     contents at $C8D3
```

After the instruction is executed, the the accumulator contains $4F.

```
                  ------------
                  !     !     !
   contents-->    ! B1  ! 70  !
                  !     !     !
                  ------------
   address--->   1200  1201  1202
```

In pseudo-BASIC it looks like:

```
A =  PEEK ( PEEK($70) + 256 * PEEK($71) + Y )
```

Indirect indexed addressing is indicated by placing the operand in parentheses. This addressing mode is very efficient, because you can access the entire memory with a two-byte instruction. This mode is used for managing tables and loops. It is more flexible than the simple indexed addressing, because the entire memory range can be addressed, not just the memory in a single page. Only the contents of the two-byte pointer in the zero page need be changed.

7) Indexed Indirect Addressing

Another addressing mode is the indexed indirect address mode, in contrast to the above indirect indexed addressing mode. It works with the X-register instead of the Y-register. Here also the address is formed from two consecutive zero-page locations. When calculating the address, the index is first added to the pointer and then the contents are used as a pointer to the actual address. An example:

```
LDA ($70,X) (X)   =>  $08    contents of X register
            $70   =>  $78    added to zero-page addr
     =>   ($78)   =>  $40    contents of $78
          ($79)   =>  $20    contents of $20
                     $2040   yields this address
        ($2040)   =>  $A9    contents at $2040
```

The accumulator contains $A9 after the instruction is executed.

```
                -------------
                !    !     !
contents-->     ! A1 !  08 !
                !    !     !
                -------------
address--->    1200  1201  1202
```

In pseudo-BASIC it looks like this:

A = PEEK (PEEK($70 + X) + 256*PEEK($70 + X + 1))

First the contents of the X-register is added to the operand and the contents of the resulting address is used a pointer to the actual address. The indexed indirect address mode is seldom used in contrast to the indirect indexed mode. You will probably have little occasion to use this mode at the beginning.

Here is a summary of the addressing modes and operation codes:

Address mode	LDA	LDX	LDY	
immediate	$A9	$A2	$A0	operation codes
absolute	$AD	$AE	$AC	
zero page	$A5	$A6	$A4	
absolute X-indexed	$BD	-	$BC	
absolute Y-indexed	$B9	$BE	-	
zero-page X-indexed	$B5	-	$B4	
zero-page Y-indexed	-	$B6	-	
indirect indexed	$B1	-	-	
indexed indirect	$A1	-	-	

The relative addressing mode and the accumulator addressing mode are discussed later.

B. The STORE Instructions

The counterparts of the load instructions are the store instructions. Using these instructions we can place the contents of a register into memory. The mnemonics for the instructions are:

STA
STX
STY

The contents of the accumulator, X-register or Y-register are placed in the appropriate memory location, which is specified by the operand that follows the instruction code. The same addressing modes used for the load instructions apply to these instructions except for the immediate mode. Storing the contents of a register changes neither the register nor the status flags.

Here are the operation codes and addressing modes:

Address mode	STA	STX	STY	
absolute	$8D	$8E	$8C	operation codes
zero page	$85	$86	$84	
absolute X-indexed	$9D	-	-	
absolute Y-indexed	$99	-	-	
zero-page X-indexed	$95	-	$94	
zero-page Y-indexed	-	$96	-	
indirect indexed	$91	-	-	
indexed indirect	$81	-	-	

You should already be acquainted with the BASIC command corresponding to the store instructions: the POKE command. It writes the contents of a variable to a specified address in memory. In pseudo-BASIC, the equivalents might look like this:

```
STA $8000         POKE $80A
STX $C020,Y       POKE $C020+Y,X
STY $F1           POKE $F1,Y
```

Store instructions are either two or three bytes in length depending on the addressing mode used. The address modes are the same as for the load instructions. The flags are not affected by store instructions.

With the load and store instructions, you are now acquainted with two important groups of instructions which serve to communicate between the microprocessor and the memory.

C. The Transfer Instructions

The 6510 microprocessor has instructions to copy the contents of one register to another. You can, for example, transfer the contents of the X-register into the accumulator or vice versa. This is quite important because many instructions only work with the accumulator. After executing these instructions, the contents of the source register are unchanged; the value is merely copied into the destination register. The transfer instructions within the processor require the participation of the accumulator; a direct transfer from the X to Y register or vice versa is not possible.

All transfer instructions are one-byte instructions; they need no operand.

Below are the individual transfer instructions and the pseudo-BASIC commands.

```
TAX       X = A
```

The contents of the accumulator is copied into the X register. The Z and N flags are affected, but the original contents of the accumulator remain unchanged.

```
TXA       A = X
```

The contents of the X-register is copied into the accumulator. The N and Z flags are affected. The contents of the X-register are unchanged.

```
TAY        Y = A
TYA        A = Y
```

These are the corresponding instructions for the Y-register. They work exactly like the above instructions, but substituting the Y-register for the X register.

The next two transfer instructions affect the stack pointer. They are seldom used, although the stack pointer is discussed later. The stack pointer can be exchanged only with the X-register.

```
TSX        X = SP
```

The contents of the stack pointer is placed into the X-register. The Z and N flags are set according to the value. The contents of the stack pointer remain unaltered by this operation.

```
TXS        SP = X
```

The contents of the X-register are placed into the stack pointer. No flags are affected by this instruction. The contents of the X-register are unaltered.

All the transfer instructions are contained in this table, along with their instruction codes.

Command	Op code
TAX	$AA
TXA	$8A
TAY	$A8
TYA	$98
TSX	$BA
TXS	$9A

D. The Arithmetic Instructions

As with most 8-bit microprocessors, the 6510 can perform only two arithmetic operations - addition and subtraction. Multiplication and division must be implemented by the user. Each calculation requires two operands which are combined to produce a result. For the 6510, the first operand is contained in the accumulator and the second operand is obtained from memory. The various addressing modes are used for this. The result of the arithmetic operation is always left in the accumulator. The comparisons with the corresponding pseudo-BASIC commands makes this clearer.

First consider addition. The contents of the addressed memory location are added to the accumulator and the result is again placed back in the accumulator.

```
ADC #$3A          A = A + $3A
```

If you add two 8-bit values (0 to 255), the result may not be able to be represented by an 8-bit number. An overflow may occur. Let's take a look at the binary addition:

```
ADC #$3A; the accumulator contains $9E.

        $9E  =  %10011110
        $3A  =  %00111010
```

The addition looks like this:

```
     10011110      $9E
   + 00111010     +$3A
  -----------     ----

     10111000  =  $D8
```

Binary addition is carried out in the same manner as decimal addition. Four different results are possible in binary addition:

```
0 + 0 = 0
0 + 1 = 1
1 + 0 = 1
1 + 1 = 0 plus overflow
```

A carry, as in decimal addition, is taken into account in the next position. In our example, we get %10111000 or $D8 as the answer. The result can be represented in eight bits. Here is another example:

```
ADC #$3A
```

The accumulator now contains $E4. The addition looks like this:

```
       11100100      $E4
   +   00111010     +$3A
  ------------      ----

      100011110  =  $11E
```

Here the result overflows 8 bits; the answer is %100011110 or $11E. But the accumulator holds only an 8-

bit number. So the carry flag is used to indicate an overflow. After each addition, overflow is indicated by the carry flag. If an overflow occurs, the carry flag is set (to 1); if no overflow occurs, the carry flag is cleared (to 0).

You can think of the carry flag as the ninth bit of the accumulator. If you want to add numbers which cannot be represented in 8-bits, multi- precision addition is used. A 16-bit number (two 8-bit memory locations) can represent numbers between 0 and 65535.

To add two 16-bit numbers, add the low-bytes of each operand and then the high-bytes of each operand. If an overflow occurs during the addition of the low-bytes, the carry flag adjusts for this during the addition of the high-bytes. Remember to clear the carry flag before adding the low-bytes so that the previous contents of the carry flag do not affect the addition. Here is an example of adding two numbers NUM1 and NUM2 with the result being placed in SUM:

```
CLC                      ;clear carry flag
LDA   NUM1LOW            ;low half of NUM1
ADC   NUM2LOW            ;low half of NUM2
STA   SUMLOW             ;low half of result
LDA   NUM1HIGH           ;high half of NUM1
ADC   NUM2HIGH           ;high half of NUM2
STA   SUMHIGH            ;high half of result
```

Now we can give the equivalent instruction in pseudo-BASIC.

```
ADC #$3A        A = A + $3A + C
```

Any overflow is indicated by the carry flag after each addition. Besides the carry flag, the zero and negative flags are also affected, depending on whether the result is zero or the seventh bit is set. An additional flag, the V flag, is used for signed arithmetic. The following table contains the operation codes for the ADC instruction in the various addressing modes.

Address mode	ADC	
immediate	$69	operation codes
absolute	$6D	
zero page	$65	
absolute x-indexed	$7D	
absolute y-indexed	$79	
zero-page x-indexed	$75	
indirect indexed	$71	
indexed indirect	$61	

Subtraction is performed in much the same way as addition. The contents of the addressed memory location is subtracted from the accumulator and the result is left in the accumulator. It is possible that the result cannot be represented in 8-bits. With subtraction, an overflow cannot occur, only an underflow. In this case, the result is less than zero. The carry flag indicates this too. Since overflow and underflow have opposite meanings, underflow is indicated by carry flag being cleared. A carry flag being set means that no underflow has occurred. Correspondingly, the carry flag must be set prior to subtraction (or the first byte of multi-precision subtraction). For example:

```
SEC                ;set carry flag for subtraction
LDA   VAL1         ;subtrahend
SBC   VAL2         ;minuend
BCC   NEGATIVE     ;carry clear means VAL2>VAL1
BCS   NOTNEG       ;carry set means VAL2<=VAL1
        .
        .
```

In pseudo-BASIC we can formulate this as follows:

```
SBC #$3A        A = A - $3A - (1-C)
```

Binary subtraction is executed in a manner similar to addition. There are four possible cases:

```
0 - 0 = 0
0 - 1 = 1  plus underflow
1 - 0 = 1
1 - 1 = 0
```

If the accumulator contains $7F, the binary representation looks like this:

```
$7F   %01111111
$3A   %00111010
```

After setting the carry flag, the subtraction looks like

this:

```
        01111111
      - 00111010
    ------------
        01000101
```

The result is %01000101 or $45. Since no underflow occurs, the carry flag is set again. The next example is somewhat different. This time the accumulator contains $1E and the carry flag is set.

```
$1E   %00011110
$3A   %00111010
```

The subtraction yields the following:

```
        00011110
      - 00111010
    ------------
        11100100
```

The result is %11100100 or $E4. Because an underflow occurred, the carry flag is cleared. How is this result interpreted? Consider how we do subtraction using decimal numbers. In decimal, our calculation is 30-58. The answer is a negative number, -28. In this example, the register contains $E4 or 228 (decimal). How are these number related? If we subtract the result from 256, so we get 28. The cleared carry flag after subtraction tells us that the result must be interpreted as a negative number.

Negative numbers are represented using **two's complement** notation. To find the two's complement of a number, invert all of the bits of the binary number and then add one to this result.

```
        11100100   original number
  gives 00011011   invert each bit
      + 00000001   plus 1
      ----------
        00011100   gives two's complement
```

The result is %00011100 or $1C or 28 in decimal.

Note that the carry flag must be cleared before addition. After addition, a set carry flag indicates an overflow. The carry flag must be set before subtraction. After subtraction, a clear carry flag indicates underflow and the result is in two's complement representation.

This table contains the operation codes for the addressing modes.

Address mode	SBC	
immediate	$E9	operation code
absolute	$ED	
zero page	$E5	
absolute x-indexed	$FD	
absolute y-indexed	$F9	
zero-page x-indexed	$F5	
indirect indexed	$F1	
indexed indirect	$E1	

E. The logical instructions

The logical instructions combine two value with each other. As with the arithmetic instructions, one operand must be in the accumulator while the second is retrieved from memory according to the addressing mode. After the operation, the result is left in the accumulator. The 6510 can perform three different types of logical operations.

The AND instruction

The AND operation compares each bit of the accumulator with the corresponding bit in the operand. If the bit of the accumulator AND the corresponding bit of the operand are both set (to 1), the corresponding bit of the result is also set to one.

```
0 AND 0 = 0
0 AND 1 = 0
1 AND 0 = 0
1 AND 1 = 1
```

The bit-wise comparison of the accumulator and operand can be made clearer with an example.

```
AND #$37
```

Say, that the accumulator contains $5D. ANDing the accumulator with $37 gives the following:

```
$5D   01011101
$37   00110111
      --------
$15   00010101
```

The result is %00010101 or $15. This corresponds exactly to the pseudo-BASIC instruction AND:

```
A = A AND $37
```

In this case, A = $5D AND $37 or A = 93 AND 55. We get the answer 21 or $15. The AND operation affects the N and Z flags. A result of zero sets the Z flag, while results greater than $7F (127) set the N flag.

This table contains the operation codes for each addressing

Address mode	AND	
immediate	$29	operation codes
absolute	$2D	
zero page	$25	
absolute x-indexed	$3D	
absolute y-indexed	$39	
zero-page x-indexed	$35	
indirect indexed	$31	
indexed indirect	$21	

The OR instruction

The OR instruction compares each bit of the accumulator with the corresponding bits of the operand. If a bit of the accumulator OR a corresponding bit of the operand equals 1, the corresponding bit of the result is set to one.

```
0 ORA 0 = 0
0 ORA 1 = 1
1 ORA 0 = 1
1 ORA 1 = 1
```

You can see from the value table that this is the "inclusive" OR. The result is one if the first operand and/or the second operand is one, not in the sense of either/or (but not both). The OR instruction affects the N and Z flags. Here's an example:

```
ORA #$37
```

The accumulator contains $5D. ORing the accumulator with $37 works like this:

```
$5D   01011101
$37   00110111
      ---------
$7F   01111111
```

The result is %01111111 or $7F. This corresponds exactly to the BASIC instruction OR:

A = A OR $37

in our case, A = $5D OR $37 or A = 93 OR 55. We get 127 or $7F.

The table below contains the operation codes for each addressing mode.

Address mode	ORA	
immediate	$09	operation codes
absolute	$0D	
zero page	$05	
absolute x-indexed	$1D	
absolute y-indexed	$19	
zero-page x-indexed	$15	
indirect indexed	$11	
indexed indirect	$01	

The Exclusive OR instruction

The operand and the accumulator are compared bit by bit. The result is set to one if either one or the other bit is one, but not both. The truth table looks like this:

```
0 EOR 0 = 0
0 EOR 1 = 1
1 EOR 0 = 1
1 EOR 1 = 0
```

The result of the operation is one if the two bits do not equal each other. Here too the N and Z flags are affected according to the result. There is no corresponding BASIC instruction. In BASIC you have to compare all the bits individually with a loop. An example looks like this:

```
EOR #$37
```

The accumulator contains $5D. EORing the accumulator with $37 gives the following:

```
$5D  01011101
$37  00110111
     ---------
$6A  01101010
```

The result is %01101010 or $6A (106).

The table below contains the op codes for the different addressing modes:

Address mode	EOR	
immediate	$49	operation code
absolute	$4D	
zero page	$45	
absolute x-indexed	$5D	
absolute y-indexed	$59	
zero-page x-indexed	$55	
indirect indexed	$51	
indexed indirect	$41	

The BIT instruction

A special feature of the 65XX microprocessors is the BIT instruction. This instruction does not change the contents of any registers. It affects only the flags. The contents of the accumulator are ANDed with the contents of the addressed memory location. If the final result is zero, the Z flag is set, otherwise it is cleared. Additionally, the value of the sixth bit of the addressed location is placed into the V flag and the seventh bit is put in the N flag. With this one can check these two bits of a memory location without disturbing the contents of any of the registers. Let us look at an example:

```
LDA  #$10
BIT  $1234
```

The accumulator contains $10; address $1234 contains $43. The AND operation yields the following result:

```
$10    %00010000     ;contents of accumulator
$43    %01000011     ;contents of memory location $1234
AND    %00000000     ;logical result of AND
```

The AND operation produces zero, so the Z is then set. The V flag equals the sixth bit of the operand, one, while the N flag is cleared. The result is:

```
Z = 1; V = 1; N = 0.
```

Two addressing modes can be used with the BIT instruction:

```
Address mode     BIT
-------------------
zero page        $24 operation codes
absolute         $2C
```

F. The Compare instructions

These instructions compare the contents of a register and the contents of a memory location. These instructions alter neither the register nor the memory contents, affecting only the flags. You can determine the relationship of the two numbers by examining the flags.

The compare instructions work by logically "subtracting" the contents of the addressed memory contents from the contents of the register and setting the flags as if an actual subtration occurred. The register contents are not changed. The C, N, and Z flags are affected depending on the result of the "subraction". There are compare commands for the three work registers of the microprocessor.

The CMP instruction

This instruction compares the contents of the accumulator with the contents of the addressed memory location, by logically subtracting the contents of the operand from the accumulator. If an underflow occurs, the carry flag is cleared; otherwise it is set. If the result is zero, the Z flag is set; otherwise it is cleared. If the result is greater than $7F (127), the N flag is set, otherwise it is cleared. Let us take a look at an example:

```
LDA  #$50
CMP  #$30
```

The accumulator contains $50. The calculation $50 - $30 is then carried out, with a result of $20. Because no underflow occurred, the carry flag is set. The zero flag is cleared because the result is not equal to zero. The N flag is cleared because the number is not greater than $7F. We get the following result:

```
C = 1;  Z = 0;  N = 0
```

Now another example:

```
LDA  #$30
CMP  #$30
```

Since the accumulator now contains $30, the logical subtraction yields zero. The carry flag is set because no underflow occurred. Since the result is zero, the zero flag is set this time. The N flag is clear because the result is not greater than $7F.

```
C = 1; Z = 1; N = 0
```

Finally a last example:

```
LDA  #$10
CMP  #$30
```

In this example, the accumulator contains $10 and the logical subtraction yields $10 - $30 = $F0. The carry flag is cleared to indicate the underflow and the Z flag is cleared because the result is not zero. This time the N flag is set.

```
C = 0; Z = 0; N = 1
```

In practice, the flags indicate that the accumulator contents are:

```
C = 1   :  >=  greater than or equal to the operand
Z = 1   :  =   equal to the operand
C = 0   :  <   less than the operand
```

To determine if the accumulator is greater than the operand (not greater than or equal to), two flags must be checked:

```
Z = 0 and C = 1
```

The compare instructions alter only the flags; they are the basis for the conditional branch instructions described in the next section. Note that these flag interpretations are for comparing unsigned integers only.

This table contains the operation codes for each addressing mode:

Address mode	CMP	
immediate	$C9	operation codes
absolute	$CD	
zero-page	$C5	
absolute x-indexed	$DD	
absolute y-indexed	$D9	
zero-page x-indexed	$D5	
indirect indexed	$D1	
indexed indirect	$C1	

The CPX instruction

The CPX instruction works the same way as the CMP instruction. Here the contents of the addressed memory location are compared not with the contents of the accumulator, but rather with the contents of the X-register. The contents of the registers are not altered. What was said above concerning the CMP instruction applies to the CPX instruction as well. There are not as many addressing modes for the CPX instruction, however.

Address mode	CPX	
immediate	$E0	operation codes
absolute	$EC	
zero page	$E4	

The CPY instruction

These instructions are the same as the CPX instructions except that the Y-register is used in place of the X-register. There are only three addressing modes.

Address mode	CPY	
immediate	$C0	operation codes
absolute	$CC	
zero page	$C4	

G. Conditional branching instructions

Next we introduce the instructions that allow you to make programming decisions. The foundations of these decisions are the conditions of the flags. The following four flags can be used to make decisions: the Z flag, the N flag, the C flag, and the V flag.

For each flag there are two conditional branch commands: the first branches if the flag is set, the second if the flag is clear. The operand of each conditional branch instruction specifies the location where the microprocessor is to get the next operation code should the condition tested for be true.

The 6510 microprocessor uses the relative addressing mode for conditional branch instructions. The operand is not an absolute memory address, but rather an address relative to the current contents of the program counter. This relative address is an 8-bit value. The relative address is added to the contents of the program counter and the branch is made to that computed address if the condition tested for is true.

With this 8-bit value you can represent 256 different numbers, so you can branch to any of 256 possible locations. The relative address causes a branch forward if the 8-bit value is positive and causes a branch backward if the 8-bit value is negative. So relative addressing can perform backward branching by allowing the use of negative operands.

Let's talk a bit about negative numbers. Using two's complement representation all numbers having bit seven set are considered to be negative:

%10000000	$80	-128
%10000001	$81	-127
...	...	....
%11111110	$FE	-2
%11111111	$FF	-1
%00000000	$00	0
%00000001	$01	1
%00000010	$02	2
...	...	....
%01111110	$7E	126
%01111111	$7F	127

The seventh bit determines if the number is positive or negative (also the condition of the N flag). Let's look at how we can calculate the distance for a relative branch. The calculation is based on the address of the instruction following the conditional branch instruction. An example: The branch instruction is at address $C47A and we want to branch to $C4BF.

```
$C47A      address of branch instruction
$C47C      address of next instruction
  .
$C4BF      destination address
```

Now we simply find the difference between destination and

the address of the instruction following the conditional branch instruction:

```
$C4BF - $C47C  =  $43
```

The operand for our branch instruction is $43. How do we calculate the relative address for a backward branch? Say we want to branch to the address $C440. You can calculate the relative address as follows:

```
$C440 - $C47C  =  $FFC4 with underflow
```

Simply use the least significant byte - $C4 as the operand for the conditional branch instruction. You could also calculate the relative address by obtaining the positive difference and taking the two's complement of the result.

```
$C47C - $C440  =  $3C
```

The two's complement:

```
    %00111100      original value    = $3C
    %11000011      invert all bits   = $C3
  +         1      add 1
    %11000100  =   two's complement = $C4
```

Here also we get an offset of $C4.

What advantages does relative addressing have? First of

all, the branch instructions take up only two bytes in memory. Besides the savings in memory there is a faster speed of execution. A two byte instruction is executed faster by the microprocessor. The most important advantage of relative addressing is that the branch address is relative to the point of execution. Since the branch instructions do not use absolute addresses, if you place the same program segment in a different place in memory, the program does not have to be changed--the location to the branch address does not change.

If the address to branch to were given in absolute form, it would have to be changed if the program were move to a different memory location. The disadvantage of relative addressing is the limited address range to which we can branch. Only 129 bytes forward or 126 bytes backward from the branch instruction is the maximum that can be jumped. In practice this is usually no great hindrance, though, because it is seldom that a larger distance is involved.

If you have found the address calculation of relative addressing quite complicated, you can rest at ease. We have presented this discussion only so that you understand the principle. Later, the assembler will take over this work for you; you need only give it the branch destination. The assembler will bring it to your attention if you attempt to jump beyond the permitted distance.

Branch on zero flag

A branch when the zero flag is set results from the instruction "branch on equal," shortened to BEQ. If the branch is to be made on a cleared zero flag, the instruction is called "branch not equal," BNE.

Branch on carry flag

Here the instruction is called "branch on carry set" or BCS for branching on a set carry flag and "branch on carry clear", BCC, for a branch on carry clear flag.

Branch on negative flag

If the negative flag is set, the instruction "branch on minus," BMI, will branch; in order to jump on a clear negative flag, the instruction "branch on plus," BPL, must be used.

Branch on overflow flag

The overflow can also be used as the basis for conditional branches. The corresponding commands are "branch on oVerflow set," BVS, and "branch on oVerflow clear," BVC. Because of the secondary importance of the V flag, these commands are seldom used.

This table contains all commands for conditional branching, together with their op codes.

Command	Op code
BEQ	$F0
BNE	$D0
BCS	$B0
BCC	$90
BMI	$30
BPL	$10
BVS	$70
BVC	$50

H. The Jump instructions

In contrast to the conditional branch commands above, the unconditional jump instructions branches to an absolute address. These instructions are not dependent on any condition and is always executed. The destination address is specified in reverse sequence (low-byte followed by high-byte) as are the other absolute addresses.

```
JMP $C420   direct jump to location $C420
```

In addition to the absolute form of the jump instruction, there is also an indirect addressing form, a peculiarity of the jump instructions. With this instruction, the specified address is not jumped to. Instead, this address tells where to get the actual destination address. For this, two consecutive bytes are again used as a pointer, in the format low byte, high byte.

```
JMP ($0302)  indirect jump to destination pointed
                to by address $0302
```

The actual address is now taken from memory locations $0302 and $0303. If, for example, $40 and $C8 are in these locations, a branch to location $C840 will be made. This method of addressing works only with the JMP instruction. The table contains the operation codes for both addressing modes.

```
Address mode   JMP
-------------------
absolute       $4C operation codes
indirect       $6C
```

The operating system of the Commodore 64 makes use of this method of addressing. There are several addresses (called vectors) located from $300 to $33C, that contain addresses for indirect JMPs. The operating system uses these vectors for performing frequently used routines.

I. The Increment and Decrement instructions

For effective programming of loops and counters, the 6510 has commands to increment or decrement the contents of a register or memory location by one. These increment instructions correspond, together with the conditional branching commands, to the NEXT instruction in BASIC. The STEP-1 instruction can be simulated with the decrement commands.

INX

The contents of the X register are incremented by one. The N and Z flags are set according to the result. In BASIC, this instruction can be formulated:

```
X = X + 1
```

If a value of $FF is incremented, the overflow is not taken into account (the carry flag is not set). The contents are set to zero, and the Z flag is set.

INY

This is the corresponding instruction to increment the Y register. It affects the flags in the same way.

There is no instruction on the 6510 to increment or decrement the accumulator contents.

INC

This instruction increments the contents of a memory location by one. The Z and N flags are again set depending on the result. This instruction is different from the previous ones in that here the contents of a memory location is first read, then incremented by one, and then saved again (read - modify - write). The commands which you are acquainted with so far either read or wrote a memory location, but never both. The INC instruction does not alter the contents of the accumulator.

In pseudo-BASIC, we can formulate this like so:

```
POKE M, PEEK(M) + 1
```

M is the address of the memory location.

DEX

This instruction decrements the contents of the X register. When decrement from $00 to $FF, the carry flag is not set. The N and Z flags are set depending on the result. In psdueo-BASIC this can be written as

```
X = X - 1
```

DEY

This instruction is the analog of the previous instruction, decrementing the contents of Y instead of X. The flags are affected in the same manner.

DEC

With this instruction the contents of a memory cell can be decremented without losing the contents of the accumulator. Its operation is equivalent to that of the INC instruction.

Here again is the table of instructions and their opcodes:

Command	Op code
INX	$E8
INY	$C8
DEX	$CA
DEY	$88

Address mode	INC	DEC	
absolute	$EE	$CE	operation codes
zero page	$E6	$C6	
absolute x-indexed	$FE	$DE	
zero-page x-indexed	$F6	$D6	

J. Flag manipulation instructions

In addition to the instructions whose results affect the flags, the flags can also be directly set or cleared by the programmer. Sometimes this is necessary before performing addition and subtraction. These instructions do not require any operands. They are all one-byte in length.

The carry flag

The carry flag is set by the instruction SEC (set carry), and cleared by CLC (clear carry).

The SEC instruction must be used before each subtraction and the CLC instruction before each addition, otherwise the answer may be wrong.

The decimal flag

This flag determines whether the processor performs addition and subtraction in binary (indicated by a cleared flag, as we have already learned) or in binary-coded decimal (BCD). This is the case if the flag is set. The microprocessor then works with BCD numbers. The instruction SED (set decimal) sets the flag, CLD (clear decimal) clears the flag.

The interrupt flag

The I flag determines whether the processor is ready to accept an interrupt or not. If the I flag is set with SEI (set interrupt disable), no interrupts will be accepted, while if it is cleared with CLI (clear interrupt disable), the processor can accept interrupts.

The overflow flag

The V flag can only be cleared on instruction. The instruction CLV (clear oVerflow) serves this purpose.

This table contains the operation codes for these one-byte commands.

Command	Op code
CLC	$18
SEC	$38
CLD	$D8
SED	$F8
CLI	$58
SEI	$78
CLV	$B8

K. The Shift Instructions

The 6510 microprocessor has some instructions for which there are no equivalents in BASIC: the shift instructions. These instructions shift the bits in the accumulator or addressed memory location one position to the right or left. If these instructions are used in reference to the accumulator, one speaks of accumulator addressing. Depending on the addressing mode, these commands can consist of one, two, or three bytes. If a memory location is addressed, they behave as an INC or DEC instruction by following a read with a write. The contents of the accumulator remain unchanged by this addressing mode.

ASL

ASL stands for "arithmetic shift left." It shifts the of the addressed byte by one bit-position to the left. A zero is placed in the right-most bit (bit 0) and the carry flag is set equal to the left-most bit (bit 7). Let us look at an example using the accumulator.

```
ASL A       The accumulator contains $47

    $47     %01000111
            %10001110      $8E, C = 0
```

In this case, the result is $8E and the carry flag is cleared because the accumulator contains a zero in the seventh position. If we compare the contents of the accumulator before and after the shift, we notice that the accumulator has doubled. When we shift a normal decimal number one position left, we get the value times ten. With the binary system, shifting left to the next position results in only doubling the value. With the ASL instruction we have a simple method of doubling a number. Let us try another example:

```
ASL A      The accumulator contains $CD

 $CD   %11001101
       %10011010       $9A, C = 1
```

Here too we double the original value and the carry flag is set. The double of $CD (205) is therefore $19A (410).

LSR

The LSR instruction (logical shift right) corresponds to the ASL instruction; here, however, the value is shifted right. The seventh bit is loaded with zero and bit zero is placed in the carry flag.

```
LSR A      The accumulator contains $CA.
```

```
$CA   %11001010
      %01100101     $65, C = 0
```

The result is $65. The carry flag contains the value of bit position 0 before the shift occurs, in this case 0. So the carry flag is clear. You may have noticed that, shifting one bit position to the right divides the original value by two. The carry flag gives the contents of bit 0 before the shift. We can interpret the value of the carry as the remainder of the division by two. This way we can tell if a number is odd or even. The LSR instruction shifts the lowest bit into the carry. The carry flag can then be tested with BCC or BCS. If a memory location is addressed with the LSR instruction, the contents of the accumulator are retained.

ROL

With the ROL instruction (rotate left) we can shift a memory location or register left cyclically, that is, rotate the bits. The carry flag is shifted into bit 0 while the contents of bit 7 are placed in the carry. Therefore we have a cyclical shift of nine bits (8 bits of the register plus the carry flag). An example will clarify this.

```
ROL  A    The accumulator contains $4B,
          the carry flag is set.

$4B  %01001011     C=1
$97  %10010111     C=0
```

All bits are shifted one position to the left. The carry flag is transferred into the now-vacant bit 0. The pushed-out seventh bit is placed into the carry. We get a result of $97 and a cleared carry. Here again the contents of the accumulator are doubled; any overflow is placed into the carry.

ROR

The ROR instruction (rotate right) is the opposite of the ROL instruction and rotates the contents of a register cyclically one position to the right. In so doing, the contents of the carry flag are placed into the now-free position 7 while the pushed-out contents of bit 0 are placed into the carry flag.

```
    ROR  A    The accumulator contains $89,
              the carry flag is clear.

     $89  %10001001     C=0
     $44  %01000100     C=1
```

From $89 we get $44, the carry is set and indicates a remainder from the division by two. All shift and rotate commands set the N and Z flags depending on if the result greater than $7F or equal to 0.

This table contains the operation codes for all

addressing modes:

Address mode	ASL	LSR	ROL	ROR	
accumulator	$0A	$4A	$2A	$6A	operation code
absolute	$0E	$4E	$2E	$6E	
zero page	$06	$46	$26	$66	
absolute x-indexed	$1E	$5E	$3E	$7E	
zero page y-indexed	$16	$56	$36	$76	

L. The Subroutine Instructions

A very important programming technique, which you already know from BASIC, is the use of subroutines. In BASIC, the instruction GOSUB is used to call a subroutine, and the instruction RETURN is used to return from the subroutine. How is a subroutine call distinguished from a normal jump instruction such as GOTO or JMP? When we call a subroutine, the processor or BASIC interpreter must make note of the location from which the subroutine was called so that the RETURN instruction can branch back to the location following the call. The BASIC interpreter does this for us; the 6510 also handles this task for us in machine language. In spite of this, however, we should know how it works.

So that the processor knows which instruction to branch back to on a RETURN instruction, the current address of the program counter is saved when the call is made. A special storage area is reserved for this, called the stack. This stack lies from address $0100 to $01FF (256 to 511). There is something called a stack pointer so that the microprocessor knows at which address of the stack it can save a return address. We have already been introduced to the stack register. Let's take a look at what happens when a subroutine is called.

The processor takes the current contents of the program

counter (+2) and divides it into high and low bytes. The high byte is stored at address $100 plus SP. Then the contents of the stack pointer are decremented by one and the low byte is stored on the stack (address 100 + SP). Finally the stack pointer is decremented by one again. Now a branch is made to the subroutine.

When the processor encounters an RTS instruction, the opposite process takes place. The stack pointer is incremented by one and one byte is taken from the stack (address $100 + SP). This byte is used as the low-byte of the program counter. Then the stack pointer is incremented again and the high-byte of the program counter is fetched from the stack. Now the program counter points to the next instruction after the subroutine call and the program is continued there.

When values are placed on the stack, the value is first saved on the stack and then the stack pointer is decremented by one. When getting a byte back from the stack, the stack pointer is first incremented by one. The stack grows from top to bottom (from $1FF to $100). An example will explain these events.

```
$C480   JSR  $2000      SP = $FA
                     $01FA = $C4   SP=SP-1
                     $01F9 = $82   SP=SP-1
                        SP = $F8
```

Now execution branches to $2000, where for our example, there is a RETURN instruction.

```
$2000    RTS          SP = $F8
                      SP=SP+1  PCL = ($01F9) = $82
                      SP=SP+1  PCH = ($01FA) = $C4
                      SP = $FA
```

The program counter now contains $C482. This value is then incremented by one and so points to $C483, the next instruction after the subroutine call at address $C480.

The stack works on the principle "Last In--First Out" (LIFO). The value last placed on the stack is the first value to be returned. Using this principle, it is also possible to nest subroutines. If a subroutine is called from another subroutine, the first RTS instruction encountered returns the instruction following the most recent JSR instruction. The next RTS instruction then returns control to the instruction following the next most recent JSR instruction. For example:

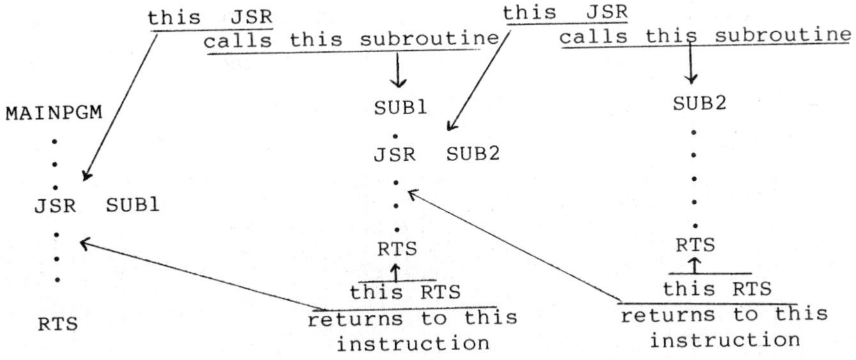

Once you become familiar with the operation of the stack, you can also use it for temporary storage of data. This is described in the next section.

The table contains the operation codes for subroutine call and return.

Command	Op code
JSR	$20
RTS	$60

M. The Stack Instructions

The 6510 has the ability to save the contents of the accumulator and the status register on the stack and to get them back again. The stack pointer is automatically decremented after writing and incremented before reading.

PHA

The instruction PHA (push accumulator) saves the contents of the accumulator on the stack and decrements the stack pointer by one. The contents of the accumulator are unchanged.

PHP

With the PHP instruction (push processor status), the entire status register (contents of the flags) is placed on the stack and the stack pointer is decremented by one. The contents of the status register are retained.

PLA

The PLA instruction (pull accumulator) is the opposite of PHA. The stack pointer is incremented and a byte read from the stack into the accumulator. The N and Z flags are set according to the value.

PLP

With this instruction, one byte is fetched from the stack and placed in the status register. This is the complement of PHP.

The table contains the operation codes.

Command	Op code
PHA	$48
PHP	$08
PLA	$68
PLP	$28

N. Instructions for handling interrupts

We are not going to use use these instructions but mention them only for the sake of completeness. The 6510 has the ability to interrupt a program from the outside world. For this, the interrupt line (IRQ, interrupt request) of the processor must be activated. The interrupt procedure is similar to a subroutine call. The processor interrupts the current program and places the contents of the program counter and the status register on the stack. Now execution branches to the address contained at $FFFE and $FFFF. The contents of these addresses are used as the new program counter.

In addition to an interruption from the outside, the 6510 can also interrupt a program through a instruction from within the program. The instruction BRK (break) serves this purpose. The program counter and the status register are saved on the stack.

In order to return to the main program from an interrupt routine, there is a instruction similar to the RTS instruction for subroutines. The instruction RTI (return from interrupt) gets the program counter and the contents of the status register back from the stack so that the program can continue without changing the flags.

The following table contains the operation codes for

these commands:

Command	Op code
BRK	$00
RTI	$40

There is one instruction which has not been mentioned yet which does absolutely nothing and so is called NOP (no operation). This instruction is used to remove operation codes from a program without shifting the rest of the commands, as well as in delay loops (this instruction too requires a certain amount of time to execute).

Command	Op code
NOP	$EA

4. Entering Machine Language Programs

Now that we have become acquainted with the instructions of the microprocessor and their functions, let's turn our thoughts to writing programs in machine language. How do we enter such programs?

As we have already seen from the descriptions of the instructions, a machine language program program consists simply of a set of instruction codes and their corresponding operands, if any. As a simple example, we will display a character on the screen of the Commodore 64. We can do this with these simple POKE commands in BASIC:

```
POKE 1024,1  : REM    DISPLAY CODE FOR A
POKE 55296,7 : REM    COLOR CODE FOR YELLOW
```

When we execute both commands, a yellow "A" appears in the upper left-hand corner of the display. Now we want to see how these two commands can be performed in machine language. For this, we recall that the POKE command can be replaced by the instruction STA. This instruction places the contents of the accumulator at the address specified by the operand. First load the accumulator with the desired value.

```
LDA  #1
STA  1024
```

Here the accumulator is loaded with the value 1 and the

contents are saved at address 1024. In the same way, we can set the value for the color code.

```
LDA  #7
STA  55296
```

If we were to try entering these instructions directly into the computer, we would get a **?SYNTAX ERROR.** The Commodore 64 normally understands only BASIC commands. These instructions are "foreign" to the BASIC interpreter. Therefore we must proceed in a different manner. Recall that a machine language program is nothing more that a group of binary instruction codes and operands in memory.

We must convert the mnemonic instructions into their corresponding binary instruction (or operation) codes. To do this, we use the table in Appendix A. For a LDA instruction using the immediate addressing mode(we want to load the accumulator with the number 1, not with the contents of memory location 1) we find that the opcode is $A9. Next follows the operand itself, 1. We are using absolute addressing for the STA instruction. The instruction is therefore $8D. The operand in this case is a memory address, saved as a 16-bit value. For this it must be divided into two 8-bit values. First comes the low-byte and then the high-byte. Separating a 16-bit value is easier to perform if we first convert the number to hexadecimal. Therefore we convert 1024 to the hexadecimal number $0400. 55296 becomes

$D800. Let's rewrite our program using hexadecimal numbers.

```
LDA #$01
STA $0400
LDA #$07
STA $D800
```

The low-byte of $0400 is $00 and the high-byte is $04. The instruction STA $0400 is represented as $8D, $00, $04. LDA #$07 STA $D800 are represented as $A9, $07, $8D, $00, $D8. Our complete program looks like this:

```
$A9, $01, $8D, $00, $04, $A9, $07, $8D, $00, $D8
```

This set of bytes must now placed in memory. Here we encounter the next problem: Where should our program be placed in memory? We must find an area which is not used by the operating system or the BASIC interpreter. For the Commodore 64 we have such an area from address 49152 to 53247 or $C000 to $CFFF. This area is 4K bytes large and will suffice even for very large machine language programs. Let's place our program in memory beginning at address 49152. We can do this with a small BASIC program. First change the hexadecimal numbers to decimal.

```
169, 0, 141, 0, 4, 169, 7, 141, 0, 216

  100 FOR I=0 TO 9
  110 READ A : POKE 49152+I,A
  120 NEXT
  130 DATA 169,0,141,0,4,169,7,141,0,216
```

When we RUN this program, the machine language program is usually placed into memory beginning at address 49152. Now we can finally execute our program. The SYS instruction is used for this in BASIC. If we give the starting address of 49152 after the SYS instruction, the program is executed from BASIC. Be careful! What happens once the processor has executed the instruction STA $D800? It gets the contents of the next memory location and interprets it as a instruction code. If it is not a legal instruction, the processor may enter an uncontrollable state and "crash." You must then turn the computer off and then on again. The program is lost and you must start over from the beginning.

Once the processor has executed the four instructions, control should be returned to the BASIC interpreter. The SYS instruction executes our program as a subroutine. We should end the program with an RTS instruction.

```
POKE 49152+10,96
```

We can place the RTS code at the end of our program. Now we can start our program with:

```
SYS 49152
```

Immediately a yellow A appears in the upper corner of the display and the computer responds with **READY.**.

Is this procedure too complicated for you? If so, then you are not alone. Ways have been found to automate this process. After all, this is why you have has a computer!

You need a program that accepts machine language instructions such as "LDA #1" and automatically converts the mnemonics to their proper operation code and writes the generated code into memory. Such a program is called an assembler. So that you can start working with an assembler from the beginning and not lose your desire by working through boring calculations and table consultations, we have written a complete assembler for you. Before we explain the operation of the assembler, we will take a look at other utility programs that can be used for machine language programming.

The first is the monitor program. A monitor permits the direct access of the memory and registers of the microprocessor. With the monitor you can examine and alter the contents of memory and registers. In addition, you can start executing a machine language program from a monitor. Most monitor programs also permit saving and loading of programs to/from cassette or disk. If you have a monitor, then you can enter your machine language programs in hex code. This is fine for small programs or changes. Often the monitor contains something called a disassembler as well. Such a program is the opposite of an assembler. The disassembler reads a program from memory and outputs it in mnemonic form; $A9, $01 are translated to LDA #$01, for example. We have also written a disassembler. It is presented later. Using this program you can disassemble not only your own programs, but parts of the operating system and BASIC interpreter as well. You can often get valuable hints by looking at other example of good programming.

4. The Assembler

Here's a small machine language program that demonstrates the advantages of an assembler over manual entry of a machine language program.

This program displays the entire character set of the Commodore 64 on the screen. We'll do this first with a BASIC program.

The Commodore 64 can display 256 different characters on the screen; the display codes range from 0 to 255. Each display code places a unique character on the screen. Using BASIC you can do this with a loop.

```
100 X = 0
110 A = X
120 POKE 1024+X, A  : REM DISPLAY CODE
130 A = 1
140 POKE 55296+X, A : REM COLOR CODE
150 X = X + 1
160 IF X <> 256 THEN 110
170 END
```

If you RUN this program, the entire character set of the Commodore 64 is displayed. Note that the time to RUN this program is about 7 seconds.

This BASIC program is written so that you can easily convert it to machine language. Now for the conversion! We'll handle it line by line. First we can use the X-register in place of the variable X:

```
100 X = 0            =>   LDX #$0
```

We can use the accumulator in place of the variable A. The next line copies the contents of the X-register into the accumulator:

```
110 A = X            =>   TAX
```

The contents of the X-register remains unchanged. Now the contents of the accumulator are place into memory at location 1024+X. Indexed addressing is used:

```
120 POKE 1024+X, A   =>   STA 1024,X
```

Next the accumulator is loaded with the color code for white, 1.

```
130 A = 1            =>   LDA #1
```

This color code is then stored in the corresponding color memory location, 55296+X. Again indexed addressing is used:

```
140 POKE 55296+X,A   =>   STA 55296,X
```

The value in the X-register is now incremented by one:

```
150 X = X + 1        =>   INX
```

The next conversion is not as straight-forward:

```
160 IF X <> 256 THEN 110   =>  ?
```

This BASIC statement requires some consideration. We want to branch back to line 110 if the contents of X is not equal to 256. But the X-register can hold values only up to 255. What happens when the X-register contains 255 and an INX instruction (in line 150) is executed? Incrementing from 255 ($FF) we get $100. The overflow is simply ignored and the result is $00--zero.

How can we recognize this case? Recall the discussion concerning the flags. Each time the X-register is incremented, the N and Z flags are also affected. After the INX instruction, if the value in the X-register is greater than $7F (127), the N flag is set, otherwise it is cleared. Similarly if the value in the X-register is zero after the INX instruction, the Z flag is set, otherwise it is cleared. So can use the contents of the zero flag as the basis of our decision. If it is not set, the contents are not equal to 256 (0) and we must branch back to line 110.

```
160 IF X <> 256 THEN 110     =>  BNE  line 110
```

Here's another problem. In machine language programming we cannot say "branch to line 110". Instead we must specify the memory address at which the instruction in line 110 is located.

We do not know what the address is yet. We must determine the program starting address and the length of each instruction. If we begin the program at address 49152 or $C000, then these are the addresses of each instruction:

LINE#	ADDRESS	MNEMONIC
100	$C000	LDX #0
110	$C002	TXA
120	$C003	STA $0400,X
130	$C006	LDA #1
140	$C008	STA $D800,X
150	$C00B	INX
160	$C00C	BNE $C002
170	$C00E	RTS

How did we do this? First set a "program counter" to the starting address of the program. In this case it starts at $C000. Now find the length of each instruction by looking in Appendix D. The length is either one, two or three bytes. Update the "program counter" by adding the length of the instruction. The "program counter" now contains the address of the next instruction. Repeat this for each instruction.

After hand assembling the program, we find that the instruction at line 160 must branch to address $C002. Now take the trouble to convert the program to generate the machine code. Here's the code:

```
100    $C000    A2 00       LDX $0
110    $C002    8A          TXA
120    $C003    9D 00 04    STA $0400,X
130    $C006    A9 01       LDA #1
140    $C008    9D 00 D8    STA $D800,X
150    $C00B    E8          INX
160    $C00C    D0 ??       BNE $C002
170    $C00E    60          RTS
```

We can substitute the operation code for the mnemonic according to APPENDIX A. We must convert the 16-bit absolute addresses found in line 120 and 140 to their reverse forms (00 04 and 00 D8). Next we must calculate the missing offset for the branch instruction in line 160. To do this, first form the positive difference between the addresses and form the two's complement of the result.

```
   $C00E
 - $C002
--------
   $000C

$0C  =  %00001100  original value
        %11110011  invert all bits
     +          1  add 1
     ------------
$F4     %11110100  two's complement
```

We find that the offset is $F4. Enter this value as the operand of the BNE instruction above.

We have completed the hand assembly of this program. To test the program, the machine language program has to be in memory. You have to write the operation codes into memory somehow such as POKing them.

Here's an example:

```
100 REM SAMPLE ML PROGRAM TO DISPLAY CHARACTERS ON SCREEN
150 ML = 49152
200 FOR I = 0 TO 14
210 READ OC
220 POKE ML+I,OC
230 NEXT I
240 END
300 DATA 160,   0, 138, 157,   0,   4, 169,   1
310 DATA 157,   0, 216, 232, 208, 244, 96
```

Run the BASIc program to put the machine language routine in memory beginning at 49152. Now to test it, move the cursor to the lower half of the screen and enter:

SYS 49152

Almost immediately, the entire character set appears on the screen. The program which took more than seven seconds to run in BASIC now runs in a fraction of a second. It is an impressive demonstration of the speed which can be attained with machine language.

Now let's use the LEA (Lothar Englisch Assembler - named after the author) to enter machine language programs. An assembler makes machine language programming quicker, easier and less prone to error. Using the LEA, you can enter machine language programs into the computer in exactly the same way as you enter BASIC programs. You can add, delete or insert or change lines just as in BASIC. The listing for the LEA is at the end of this chapter.

A program line is called a **source statement.** When using the LEA, the source statement always begins with a line number. It also has: an optional label (more about this shortly); the mnemonic code for the machine language instruction (LDA, STA, etc.); any required or optional operand(s); and optional comments. By using comments within your assembler source program, you can describe the purpose of each instruction. Comments are denoted with a semicolon and are ignored by the assembler, but appear in the listing for your own information. They correspond to the BASIC command REM.

A complete line of assembler source for the LEA might look like this:

```
100 TEXT LDA $70,X   ;GET START VALUE
```

A complete LEA source program can also be SAVEd to disk, just like BASIC. The LEA requires you to distinguish this source program from the machine language program that it later creates by suffixing **.SRC** to the name. After you create your assembler source file, you then load the LEA assembler. Once started with RUN, LEA asks for the name of the program to be assembled (the one you just SAVEd). The LEA reads this program from the disk and creates the machine code program from it, which it places directly in memory.

In addition, the LEA produces an optional assembly listing containing the line numbers, source statement instructions including comments and generated machine codes in hexadecimal format. When assembling, the LEA automatically calculates the addresses and offsets for branches. You as the programmer, need give the branch destination not as an absolute address, but symbolically in the form of a label (also called symbol). Our example program from before looks like this:

```
100          LDX #0
110   LOOP   TXA
120          STA $0400,X
130          LDA #1
140          STA $D800,X
150          INX
160          BNE LOOP
170          RTS
```

Here we simply give a label to the address that we want to refer to later. In this case we used the symbol **LOOP.** As the assembler processes the source program, it encounters a label. It makes note of the label, LOOP, and the value the program counter at which the label (or symbol) is found. In our example, the program counter has the value $C002 at line 110. The assembler assigns this value to the symbol **LOOP.** Later, the offset for the branch instruction can be calculated from the immediate value of the program counter and the value of the symbol. As the assembler works its way through the source program, it automatically places the operation code for the mnemonic instructions and their operands in memory so that the machine language program is ready to be executed at the end of the assembly.

Using this technique, it is possible that you might refer to a label before it is defined:

```
100         LDA $40
110         BEQ CONT
120         LDX #$FF
130 CONT    STX $D840
140         RTS
```

In this program line 110 refers to a label (CONT) which at that point is not yet defined. The assembler has no way of knowing the value of the symbol **CONT.** So the assembler is designed to go though the source program twice. The first time through, the LEA makes note of all the symbols and their values. The second time through, it does the actual assembling or code generation. So during the second time through, when the LEA comes to line 110, it already knows the value of CONT from the first time through and can calculate the offset for the branch instruction.

Since the LEA assembler reads the source program twice, it is said to be a **2-pass** assembler. So that you can see the progress of the assembler, the LEA displays the number of the line it is currently working on.

When you enter a source program by using the built-in BASIC line editor, the BASIC interpreter searches through the source statements for BASIC command keywords. When it finds them, it converts these into one-byte codes called **tokens.** As a result, the LEA assembler cannot normally recognize words that contain BASIC keywords such as ON, TO, and even = and * because they have been converted to tokens. For this reason, you must first enter and RUN the following BASIC program, called **UNTOKEN** before using the BASIC line editor to create the assembler source file. UNTOKEN inhibits BASIC from tokenizing normal BASIC keywords. Thus BASIC keywords are not be converted to their corresponding tokens. This enables the LEA to recognize their untokenized equivalents in normal text.

When you are finished using the LEA, and you want to enter normal BASIC programs again, enter the instruction:

SYS 53181

This re-enables BASIC to tokenize its keywords.

```
  0 REM    PROGRAM  UNTOKEN
100 FOR I = 53100 TO 53191
110 READ X : POKE I,X : S=S+X : NEXT
120 DATA 169,119,160,207,141,  2,  3,140,  3,  3, 96, 32
130 DATA  96,165,134,122,132,123, 32,115,  0,170,240,243
140 DATA 162,255,134, 58,144,  6, 32,121,165, 76,225,167
150 DATA  32,107,169,160,  0,162,  0,189,  0,  2,232,201
160 DATA  32,240,248,201, 48,144,  4,201, 58,144,240,153
170 DATA   0,  2,201,  0,240,  7,189,  0,  2,200,232,208
180 DATA 242,200,200,200,200,200, 76,162,164,169,131,160
190 DATA 164,141,  2,  3,140,  3,  3, 96
200 IF S <> 11096 THEN PRINT "ERROR IN DATA !!" : END
210 SYS 53100 : PRINT "OK"
```

After you key in this program, you should save a copy on each diskette on which you will later store assembler source programs. Remember to load and RUN **UNTOKEN** before creating assembler source programs.

Now enter the earlier sample program. Insert line 180 which contains **.EN.** This is a pseudo-instruction which tells the assembler that this statement is at the end of your source program. Save the source program on disk with the name **TEST.SRC.**

Did you remember to first LOAD and RUN the above **UNTOKEN** program? Now you can load the LEA assembler and RUN it. The following appears on the screen. Respond as requested.

```
          6510 - ASSEMBLER

  SOURCE FILE NAME ? TEST
  LISTING Y/N      ? Y
  PRINTER Y/N      ? N
```

After a short time the message **PASS 1** appears on the screen and the disk drive shows some activity. Now the line numbers from 100 to 180 appear on the screen. During the second pass, the listing is displayed:

```
  PASS 2
    C000  A2 00        100         LDX   #0
    C002  8A           110  LOOP   TXA
    C003  9D 00 04     120         STA   $0400,X
    C006  A9 01        130         LDA   #1
    C008  9D 00 D8     140         STA   $D800,X
    C00B  E8           150         INX
    C00C  D0 F4        160         BNE   LOOP
    C00E  60           170         RTS
                       180         .EN

  LABEL  C002
```

When the listing is completed, the LEA assembler asks you if the generated machine language program should be saved to diskette. Answer with Y(es).

```
SAVE  Y/N     ? Y
```

The program is saved to diskette under the name **TEST.OBJ** on the diskette (OBJ = OBJect program). Statistics about the generated code and errors are also displayed:

```
C000 / C00F / 000F
SOURCE FILE IS TEST.SRC
0  ERRORS
```

The assembler offers the option of displaying all the symbols and their values.

```
SYMBOL TABLE  Y/N ? Y
SORT  Y/N ? N

LOOP   C002
```

You can also specify that the table is to be sorted alphabetically.

The generated machine language program is now contained on the diskette with the name **TEST.OBJ.** There is also a copy of it in memory, ready to be executed. Now test it out by entering:

SYS 49152

The entire character set appears on the screen almost immediately.

There are a few things about the assembler you should know. Each line of the source program consists of a line number, an optional symbol (also called label), and a mnemonic instruction such as LDA, followed by the operands (if necessary) and comments separated by a semicolon. The comments may be omitted of course, but we advise you to make liberal use of these and describe exactly the operations you intend. Should you lay your program aside and need to use or change it at a later time, you will be thankful that you commented it.

The symbols may be maximum of five characters in length. In addition to the implicit symbol definitions (labels), you can assign values to symbols directly. This makes programs easier to understand and easier to read.

In this example, we use symbols for the addresses of the color and screen memory:

```
PASS 2
  0400                  70 VIDEO   =      $400
  D800                  80 COLOR   =      $D800
  C000                  90         *=     $C000
  C000  A2 00          100         LDX    #0
  C002  8A             110 LOOP    TXA
  C003  9D 00 04       120         STA    VIDEO,X
  C006  A9 01          130         LDA    #1
  C008  9D 00 D8       140         STA    COLOR,X
  C00B  E8             150         INX
  C00C  D0 F4          160         BNE    LOOP
  C00E  60             170         RTS
                       180         .EN
```

If you assemble this program and display the sorted symbol table, you will see:

```
COLOR  D800        LOOP   C002
VIDEO  0400
```

Line 70 contains a pseudo-instruction = which directs the assembler to assign the value $0400 to the symbol VIDEO. Anytime you use the symbol VIDEO, the assembler knows to use the value $0400 to calculate the operands.

Line 90 contains another pseudo-instruction, ***=**. It tells the assembler to begin the assembly process at memory location $C000. It is placed at the start of each program. Using it, you can instruct the assembler to place your code at any desired place in memory.

What are the advantages of using symbols? There are two main advantages. First, through the choice of name, the purpose of an individual memory location can be easily determined (e.g. COLOR). Second, such a program is easier to change. If you enter the wrong location of the video RAM, you need only change the value of VIDEO at the beginning of the program. All references to this name are then changed. This is even more useful the more times such a name appears in a program.

A pseudo-instruction, gives processing directions to the assembler. For example, the pseudo-instruction **.BY,** tells the assembler to place specific values in the machine language program. You can, for example, store data or text within your machine language program. The pseudo-instruction for this is called:

.BY

An operand in the range from 0 to 255 must follow the **.BY** pseudo-instruction. This operand value is placed at the current location of the program counter. Using **.BY**, you can insert symbols and constants into the program. For example:

```
.BY 100
.BY $7F
.BY CR
```

.BY has an additional option. Sometimes, you have to divide a 16-bit value into two 8-bit values. The operators > and < allow you to do this. The > symbol denotes the high-byte (bits 8 through 15) of a 16-bit value, while the < symbol denotes the low-byte (bits 0 to 7). Here's an example:

```
100  CONST   =    $AB3F
110  .BY  <CONST
120  .BY  >CONST
```

This program segment places the values $3F and $AB in the program. These operators can be used for immediate addressing with the # character, for example:

```
130  LDA  #<CONST
140  LDY  #>CONST
```

In order to use zero-page addressing, you must prefix operands with an asterisk, *. If you don't, the assembler uses absolute addressing. This is not necessary for indexed addressing which works only with zero-page addresses.

```
00B0               100 START  =      $B0
C000   AD B0 00    110        LDA    START
C003   A4 B0       120        LDY    *START
C005   8D 27 00    130        STA    $27
C008   84 60       140        STY    *$60
C00A   24 B0       150        BIT    *START
```

The above example shows you that without the asterisk (lines 110 and 130), an absolute addressing mode, three-byte form of the instruction is generated. The zero-page addressing mode is selected by placing the asterisk in front of the operand, resulting in a two-byte instruction (lines 120, 140 and 150).

Now that you are acquainted with the functions of the LEA assembler, you can concentrate on programming. On the next pages you find the listing of the LEA assembler and a short description of the operations and the variables used by the program.

Try not to key the listing "blindly". Read the description of the routines as you go along, and try to understand how the assembler works. By doing this, you can learn not only about the operation of the assembler, but also something about machine language as well.

You can also order a diskette containing the LEA assembler, 6510 Single-Step Simulator and Disassembler. This saves you the time and effort of keying these programs from the listings. See ordering instructions in APPENDIX F.

```
100 REM 6510 ASSEMBLER
110 PRINT CHR$(147):PRINT:PRINT:PRINT,"6510 ASSEMBLER":PRINT:DG=8
120 INPUT"SOURCE FILE NAME ";SN$
130 IFRIGHT$(SN$,4)=".SRC"THENSN$=LEFT$(SN$,LEN(SN$)-4)
140 DD$="0":REM DRIVE NUMBER
150 INPUT"LISTING  Y/N    ";A$:IFA$<>"Y"THENPM=1:GOTO190
160 PF=4:PG=3
170 INPUT"PRINTER  Y/N    ";A$:IFA$="Y"THENPG=4
180 OPENPF,PG
190 GOSUB5000:REM BUILD TABLES
200 A=0:AD=49152:PRINT:PRINT:PA=A
210 PRINT"PASS 1":GOSUB4000:PRINT"PASS 2":FF%=0:FE%=0
220 OP$=DD$+":"+SN$+".SRC"
230 OPEN8,DG,0,OP$
240 GET#8,A$,A$:REM START ADDRESS
250 IFPM=1THENPRINTCHR$(145),,ZN$
260 F%=0:IFAD>65535THENPRINT:PRINT:PRINT"MEMORY OVERFLOW!":GOTO1000
270 A=AD:GOSUB3240:PR$=A$+"  ":GOSUB2000:IFLEFT$(X$,3)=".EN"THEN1000
280 XX$=LEFT$(X$,1):IFXX$="*"THENPR$="                  ":LN$="     "
290 IFXX$="."ORXX$="*"ORXX$="="THENGOSUB2900:GOTO380
295 IFXX$=""THENPR$=PR$+"           ":GOTO430
300 ONLM%GOTO320
310 SA=OF+AD:PA=AD:LM%=1
320 XX$=LEFT$(X$,3):FORJ=0TONN%:IFXX$=MN$(J)THEN350
330 NEXT
340 FL$(1)="A":A%=1:F%=1:GOSUB1520:GOTO370
350 GOSUB2400:F%=0:IFT%=5ANDT%(J,9)>0THENT%=9:REM RELATIVE
360 ONT%+1GOSUB500,600,600,600,600,800,800,800,500,900,600,600,800
370 POKE OF+AD,A
380 AD=AD+A%:IFLEFT$(X$,2)="*="THEN400
390 LX=AD
400 REM        ******** OUTPUT
410 IFF%=0THENIFFL$(0)=" "ANDFL$(1)=" "ANDFL$(2)=" "THEN430
420 BS%=BS%+1
430 ONPMGOTO250
440 Y$=LEFT$(Y$+"           ",11):FORI=1TO3:PRINT#PF,FL$(I);:NEXT
450 PRINT#PF,PR$ZN$LN$"  "LEFT$(X$+"      ",6)Y$" "RM$
460 GOTO 250
500 REM ONE-BYTE COMMANDS
510 A%=1:A=T%(J,T%):IFA<0THENFL$(2)="A":GOTO1510
520 GOSUB3240:PR$=PR$+RIGHT$(A$,2)+"       ":RETURN
600 REM TWO-BYTE COMMANDS
610 A=T%(J,T%):IFA<0THENFL$(2)="A":GOTO1500
620 GOSUB3240:PR$=PR$+RIGHT$(A$,2)
630 YY$=YA$:IFLEFT$(YY$,1)="#"THENYY$=MID$(YY$,2)
640 IFLEFT$(YY$,1)="*"THENYY$=MID$(YY$,2)
650 A%=2:IFLEFT$(YY$,1)=">"ORLEFT$(YY$,1)="<"THENYY$=MID$(YY$,2)
660 A$=LEFT$(YY$,1):IFA$="$"ORA$>"/"ANDA$<":"THENA$=YY$:GOTO690
670 SL$=YY$:GOSUB4500
680 A$="$"+HE$
690 GOSUB3100
700 IFLEFT$(YA$,2)="#>"THENA=INT(A/HI)
710 IFLEFT$(YA$,2)="#<"THENA=A-INT(A/HI)*HI
720 IFA>LOTHENFL$(2)="O":F%=1:A=0
730 GOSUB3240:POKEOF+AD+1,AL%:PR$=PR$+" "+RIGHT$("00"+A$,2)+"    "
740 A=T%(J,T%):RETURN
```

```
800 REM THREE-BYTE COMMANDS
810 A%=3
820 A=T%(J,T%)
830 GOSUB3240:PR$=PR$+RIGHT$(A$,2)
840 A$=LEFT$(YA$,1):IFA$="$"ORA$>"/"ANDA$<":"THENA$=YA$:GOTO870
850 SL$=YA$:GOSUB4500
860 A$="$"+HE$
870 GOSUB3100:GOSUB3240:PR$=PR$+" "+RIGHT$("OO"+A$,2)+" "+LEFT$
(A$,2)+"  "
880 POKEOF+AD+1,AL%:POKEOF+AD+2,AH%
890 A=T%(J,T%):RETURN
900 REM RELATIVE
910 A%=2
920 A=T%(J,T%):GOSUB3240:PR$=PR$+RIGHT$(A$,2)
930 A$=LEFT$(Y$,1):IFA$="$"ORA$>"/"ANDA$<":"THENA$=Y$:GOTO960
940 SL$=Y$:GOSUB4500
950 A$="$"+HE$
960 GOSUB3100:IFFL$(2)="U"THENA=AD+2
970 DF=A-(AD+2):IFDF<-128ORDF>127THENFL$(3)="R":F%=1:DF=0
980 A=DFANDLO:GOSUB3240
990 PR$=PR$+" "+RIGHT$(A$,2)+"       ":POKEOF+AD+1,A:A=T%(J,T%):RETURN
1000 PR$="                 ":IFF%=0THEN1020
1010 BS%=BS%+1
1020 IFAE<AD+OFTHENAE=AD+OF
1030 ONPMGOTO1060
1040 FORI=0TO3:PRINT#PF,FL$(I);:NEXT
1050 PRINT#PF,PR$,ZN$,LN$" "LEFT$(X$+"      ",6)Y$" "RM$
1060 CLOSE8:INPUT"SAVE  Y/N    ";A$:IFA$<>"Y"THEN1130
1070 A$=DD$+":"+SN$+".OBJ"
1080 A%=LEN(A$):POKE183,A%:POKE187,681ANDLO:POKE188,681/HI
1090 FORI=1TOA%:POKE680+I,ASC(MID$(A$,I)):NEXT:REM FILENAME
1100 A=SA:GOSUB3240:POKE251,AL%:POKE252,AH%:REM START ADDRESS
1110 A=AE:GOSUB3240:POKE781,AL%:POKE782,AH%:REM END ADDRESS
1120 POKE780,251:SYS65496:REM SAVE
1130 A=PA:GOSUB3240:PA$=A$:A=AD:GOSUB3240:AD$=A$:A=AD-PA:GOSUB3240
1140 BA$=A$:ONPMGOTO1180
1150 PRINT#PF:PRINT#PF,PA$" / "AD$" / "BA$
1160 PRINT#PF,"SOURCE FILE IS "SN$+".SRC"
1170 PRINT#PF,BS%"ERROR(S)":PRINT#PF
1180 INPUT"SYMBOL TABLE Y/N ";Z$:IFZ$<>"Y"THEN1400
1190 MX=2:IFPG>3THENPRINT#PF,CHR$(12):MX=5
1200 INPUT"SORT  Y/N ";Z$:IFZ$="Y"THEN1300
1210 ONPMGOTO1220
1220 M%=0:P$="":FORI=LL%TOUL%
1230 IFLB$(I)="      "THEN1290
1240 P$=P$+LB$(I)+"  "+HE$(I)+"      ":M%=M%+1
1250 IFM%<>MXTHEN1290
1260 ONPMGOTO1280
1270 PRINT#PF,P$
1280 P$="":M%=0:IFI>=UL%THEN1400
1290 NEXTI:IFP$<>""THEN1260
1300 HI$=CHR$(127)+CHR$(127)+CHR$(127)+CHR$(127)+CHR$(127):F%=0
:REM SORT
1310 M%=0:SL$=HI$:FORI=LL%TOUL%:IFLB$(I)="      "THEN1340
1320 IFLB$(I)<SL$THENSL$=LB$(I):M%=I+1
1330 UL%=I
1340 NEXTI:IFF%<MXTHEN1360
1350 F%=0:IFPM=0THENPRINT#PF
1360 IFM%=0THEN1400
1370 ONPMGOTO1390
```

```
1380 PRINT#PF,SL$"  "HE$(M%-1)"      ";
1390 LB$(M%-1)="      ":F%=F%+1:GOTO1310
1400 REM
1410 IFPG=4THENPRINT#PF,CHR$(12)
1420 CLOSEPF:END
1500 POKEOF+AD+2,0:REM NOP FILLER
1510 POKEOF+AD+1,0
1520 A=0:PR$=PR$+NP$(A%):RETURN
1600 IFLEFT$(LN$,1)="."THENI=-1:RETURN
1610 IFMID$(LN$,4,1)<>" "THENI=NN%+1:RETURN
1620 MN$=LEFT$(LN$,3):REM LABEL=MNEMONIC?
1630 FORI=0TONN%:IFMN$<>MN$(I)THENNEXT
1640 RETURN
2000 GET#8,A$,B$:IFA$+B$=""THEN2290:REM LEFT ADDRESS
2010 GET#8,Z1$,Z2$
2020 ZN=ASC(Z1$+CHR$(0))+HI*ASC(Z2$+CHR$(0))
2030 ZN$=RIGHT$("    "+STR$(ZN),5)+" "
2040 GOSUB2300:IFFF%THENRETURN
2050 LN$="":X$="":Y$="":RM$="":X%=0
2060 FORI=0TO3:FL$(I)=" ":NEXTI:IFZ$="*"THEN2190
2070 IFZ$=";"THEN2280
2080 REM LABEL NAME
2090 IFZ$=" "ORFF%THENLN$=LEFT$(LN$+"     ",5):GOTO2120
2100 LN$=LN$+Z$:IFLEN(LN$)=6THENX%=1:FL$(0)="L"
2110 GOSUB2300:GOTO2090
2120 GOSUB1600:IFI<=NN%THENX$=LN$:LN$="      ":GOTO2200
2130 X%=ASC(LN$):IFX%<65ORX%>90THENFL$(0)="S"
2140 REM OPERATION
2150 GOSUB2300:IFFF%THENRETURN
2160 IFZ$<>" "THEN2190
2170 GOTO2150
2180 GOSUB2300:IFFF%THENRETURN
2190 IFZ$<>" "THENX$=X$+Z$:GOTO2180
2200 IFFF%THENRETURN
2210 IFZ$=";"THEN2280
2220 IFZ$<>" "THEN2260:REM OPERAND
2230 GOSUB2300:IFFF%THENRETURN
2240 GOTO2200
2250 GOSUB2300:IFFF%THENRETURN
2260 IFZ$<>" "THENY$=Y$+Z$:GOTO2250
2270 GOSUB2300:IFFF%THENRETURN:REM COMMENT
2280 RM$=RM$+Z$:GOTO2270
2290 X$=".EN":RM$="END ASSUMED":LN$="       ":Y$="":ZN$="       ":RETURN
2300 GET#8,Z$:FF%=Z$="":RETURN
2400 REM DETERMINE ADDRESSING MODE
2410 IFY$=""THENT%=8:RETURN:REM IMPLICIT
2420 YA$=Y$:IFLEFT$(YA$,1)="("THENYA$=MID$(YA$,2)
2430 IFRIGHT$(YA$,1)=")"THENYA$=LEFT$(YA$,LEN(YA$)-1)
2440 IFRIGHT$(YA$,3)="),Y"THENYA$=LEFT$(YA$,LEN(YA$)-3)
2450 IFRIGHT$(YA$,2)=",Y"ORRIGHT$(YA$,2)=",X"THENYA$=LEFT$(YA$,LEN
(YA$)-2)
2460 Z$=Y$:K$=LEFT$(Y$,1)
2470 IFZ$="A"THENT%=0:RETURN:REM ACCUMULATOR
2480 IFK$="#"THENT%=1:RETURN:REM IMMEDIATE
2490 IFK$="("THEN2600:REM INDIRECT
2500 ZP=K$="*":REM ZERO PAGE
2510 Z$=MID$(Y$,2+ZP)
2520 IFLEN(Z$)<2THEN2550
2530 K$=MID$(Z$,LEN(Z$)-1,1)
```

```
2540 IFK$=","THEN2570:REM INDEXED
2550 T%=5
2560 T%=T%+3*ZP:RETURN:REM ABSOLUTE OR ZERO-PAGE
2570 K$=RIGHT$(Z$,1):IFK$="X"THENT%=6:GOTO2560
2580 IFK$="Y"THENT%=7:GOTO2560
2590 T%=-1:RETURN:REM SYNTAX ERROR
2600 K$=RIGHT$(Z$,1):IFK$=")"THEN2630
2610 IFRIGHT$(Z$,2)<>",Y"THEN2590
2620 T%=11:RETURN
2630 IFMID$(Z$,LEN(Z$)-2,2)=",X"THENT%=10:RETURN
2640 T%=12:RETURN
2700 IFX$="="THEN2730:REM PSEUDO-OPS PASS 1
2710 IFLEFT$(X$,2)="*="THEN2780
2715 IFLEFT$(X$,3)=".BY"THENA%=1:RETURN
2720 A%=0:RETURN
2730 A%=0:IFY$="*"THENRETURN
2740 A%=ASC(LEFT$(LN$,1)):IFA%<65ORA%>90THENRETURN
2750 A$=LEFT$(Y$,1):IFA$<>"$"AND(A$<"0"ORA$>"9")THENRETURN
2760 A$=Y$:GOSUB3100:IFF%THENML$(HC%)=FL$(2):RETURN
2770 GOSUB3240:HE$(HC%)=RIGHT$("0000"+A$,4):RETURN
2780 A%=0:Y1$=LEFT$(Y$,1):IFY1$="$"ORY1$>"/"ANDY1$<":"THEN2800
2790 RETURN
2800 A$=Y$:GOSUB3100:IFF%THENRETURN
2810 HA=A:GOSUB3240:X%=ASC(LEFT$(LN$+CHR$(0),1)):IFX%>64ANDX%<91
THENHE$(HC%)=A$
2820 RETURN
2900 IFXX$="="THEN2940:REM PSEUDO-OPS PASS 2
2910 IFLEFT$(X$,2)="*="THEN2990
2915 IFLEFT$(X$,3)=".BY"THEN2991
2920 FL$(1)="S"
2930 A%=0:F%=1:PR$="                    ":RETURN
2940 A%=0
2950 A$=LEFT$(Y$,1)
2960 IFA$<>"*"ANDA$<>"$"AND(A$<"0"ORA$>"9")THENFL$(2)="S":GOTO2930
2970 SL$=LN$:F%=0:GOSUB4500:IFF%THENFL$(0)=FL$(2):FL$(2)=" ":GOTO2930
2980 PR$=HE$+"              ":RETURN
2990 A%=0:YZ$=LEFT$(Y$,1):IFYZ$="$"ORYZ$>"/"ANDYZ$<":"THEN3010
2991 YZ$=LEFT$(Y$,1):LH%=YZ$=">"ORYZ$="<":YA$=MID$(Y$,1-LH%)
2992 YZ$=LEFT$(YA$,1):IFYZ$="$"ORYZ$>"/"ANDYZ$<":"THENHE$=YA$:GOTO2994
2993 SL$=YA$:F%=0:GOSUB4500:HE$="$"+HE$:IFF%THENFL$(0)=FL$(2)
:FL$(2)=" "
2994 A$=HE$:GOSUB3100:IFA>LOANDLH%=0THENA=0:FL$(1)="O"
2995 IFLEFT$(Y$,1)=">"THENA=INT(A/HI)
2996 IFLEFT$(Y$,1)="<"THENA=A-INT(A/HI)*HI
2998 POKEAD,A:A%=1:GOSUB3240:PR$=PR$+RIGHT$("00"+A$,2)+"        "
:RETURN
3000 FL$(2)="S":F%=1:GOTO3030
3010 A$=Y$:GOSUB3100:IFF%THEN3030
3020 AD=A:GOSUB3240:PR$=A$+"  "
3030 PR$=PR$+"               ":RETURN
3100 REM CONVERT HEX -> DEC   A$ -> A
3110 Z$=LEFT$(A$,1):IFZ$="$"THENA$=RIGHT$(A$,LEN(A$)-1):GOTO3150
3120 IFZ$<"0"ORZ$>"9"THENFL$(2)="S":F%=1:RETURN
3130 A=VAL(A$):IFA>65535ORA<0THENFL$(2)="O":F%=1
3140 RETURN
3150 A=0:L%=LEN(A$):IFL%>4THENF%=1:FL$(2)="L":RETURN
3200 FORI=1TOL%:AA%=ASC(MID$(A$,I))-48
3210 IFAA%<0ORAA%>9THENIFAA%<17ORAA%>22THENF%=1:FL$(2)="S":RETURN
3220 IFAA%>9THENAA%=AA%-7
3230 A=A+AA%*16↑(L%-I):NEXT:RETURN
3240 AH%=A/HI:AL%=A-AH%*HI:A$=A$(AH%/16)+A$(AH%AND15)+A$(AL%/16)
+A$(AL%AND15)
```

```
3250 RETURN
4000 DIMLB$(349),HE$(349),ML$(349):HA=AD:REM CONSTRUCT ADDRESS LIST
4010 FORI=0TO349:LB$(I)="      ":HE$(I)="0000":ML$(I)=" ":NEXT
4020 OP$=DD$+":"+SN$+".SRC"
4030 OPEN8,DG,0,OP$
4040 GET#8,A$,A$:LL%=349
4050 IFST<>0THENCLOSE8:END
4060 GOSUB2000:PRINTCHR$(145),ZN$:IFLN$=""ORLEFT$(LN$,1)=" "THEN4210
4070 X%=ASC(LEFT$(LN$,1)):IFX%<65ORX%>90THEN4210
4080 GOSUB4100:GOTO4130
4090 LN$=LEFT$(LN$+"     ",5):REM GENERATE HASH CODE
4100 HC=0:FORI=1TO5
4110 HC%=ASC(MID$(LN$,I,1)):HC=HC+(HC%/10-INT(HC%/10))*10↑(6-I):NEXTI
4120 HC%=(HC/307-INT(HC/307))*300:RETURN
4130 A=HA:GOSUB3240
4140 IFLB$(HC%)<>"      "THEN4180
4150 LB$(HC%)=LN$:HE$(HC%)=A$:IFHC%>UL%THENUL%=HC%
4160 IFHC%<LL%THENLL%=HC%
4170 GOTO4210
4180 IFLB$(HC%)=LN$THENML$(HC%)="M":GOTO4210
4190 HC%=HC%+1:IFHC%<350THEN4140
4200 PRINT"SYMBOL TABLE FULL":CLOSE8:END
4210 IFX$=".EN"THENCLOSE8:RETURN
4220 XX$=LEFT$(X$,1):IFXX$="."ORXX$="*"ORXX$="="THENGOSUB2700:HA=HA+A%
:GOTO4060
4230 F%=0:XX$=LEFT$(X$,3):FORJ=0TONN%:IFXX$<>MN$(J)THENNEXT:GOTO4270
4240 GOSUB2400
4250 IFT%(J,T%)>=0THEN4280
4260 IFT%=5ANDT%(J,9)>=0THENT%=9:GOTO4280
4270 F%=1:HA=HA+1:GOTO4060
4280 HA=HA+L%(T%):GOTO4060
4500 REM        ******** SEARCH FOR LABEL
4510 X%=ASC(LEFT$(SL$,1)):IFX%<65ORX%>90THENFL$(2)="S":F%=1:HE$="0000"
:RETURN
4520 IFLEN(SL$)>5THENFL$(2)="L"
4530 SV$=LN$:LN$=SL$:GOSUB4090:SL$=LN$:LN$=SV$
4540 IFLB$(HC%)="      "ORHC%>UL%THENFL$(2)="U":F%=1:HE$="0000":RETURN
4550 IFLB$(HC%)<>SL$THEN4580
4560 HE$=HE$(HC%):IFML$(HC%)<>" "THENFL$(2)=ML$(HC%)
4570 RETURN
4580 HC%=HC%+1:GOTO4540
4590 Y1$="":Y2$="":I=1:REM DIVIDE Y$ INTO Y1$ AND Y2$
4600 IFMID$(Y$,I,1)<>","THENY1$=Y1$+MID$(Y$,I,1)
4610 IFI>LEN(Y$)THENF%=1:RETURN
4620 IFMID$(Y$,I,1)<>","THENI=I+1:GOTO4600
4630 I=I+1:IFI>LEN(Y$)THENF%=1:RETURN
4640 Y2$=Y2$+MID$(Y$,I,1):IFI=LEN(Y$)THENF%=0:RETURN
4650 I=I+1:GOTO4640
5000 READNN%:HI=256:LO=255
5010 DIM A$(15),MN$(NN%),T%(NN%,12),L%(12),FL$(3),NP$(3)
5020 FORI=0TO15:READA$(I):NEXT
5030 NP$(1)="00         ":NP$(2)="00 00      ":NP$(3)="00 00 00   "
5040 FORI=0TO12:READL%(I):NEXT
5050 FORJ=0TONN%:READMN$(J):FORJJ=0TO12:READA$:IFA$="-1"THENA=-1
:GOTO5070
5060 A=0:FORI=1TO2:X=ASC(RIGHT$(A$,I))-48:X=X+(X>9)*7:A=A+X*16↑
(I-1):NEXT
5070 T%(J,JJ)=A:NEXT:NEXT:RETURN
6000 DATA 55 :REM NUMBER OF MNEMONICS
6010 DATA 0,1,2,3,4,5,6,7,8,9,A,B,C,D,E,F
6020 DATA 1,2,2,2,2,3,3,3,1,2,2,2,3
7000 DATA ADC,-1,69,65,75,-1,6D,7D,79,-1,-1,61,71,-1
```

```
7010 DATA AND,-1,29,25,35,-1,2D,3D,39,-1,-1,21,31,-1
7020 DATA ASL,0A,-1,06,16,-1,0E,1E,-1,-1,-1,-1,-1,-1
7030 DATA BCC,-1,-1,-1,-1,-1,-1,-1,-1,-1,90,-1,-1,-1
7040 DATA BCS,-1,-1,-1,-1,-1,-1,-1,-1,-1,B0,-1,-1,-1
7050 DATA BEQ,-1,-1,-1,-1,-1,-1,-1,-1,-1,F0,-1,-1,-1
7060 DATA BMI,-1,-1,-1,-1,-1,-1,-1,-1,-1,30,-1,-1,-1
7070 DATA BIT,-1,-1,24,-1,-1,2C,-1,-1,-1,-1,-1,-1,-1
7080 DATA BNE,-1,-1,-1,-1,-1,-1,-1,-1,-1,D0,-1,-1,-1
7090 DATA BPL,-1,-1,-1,-1,-1,-1,-1,-1,-1,10,-1,-1,-1
7100 DATA BRK,-1,-1,-1,-1,-1,-1,-1,-1,00,-1,-1,-1,-1
7110 DATA BVC,-1,-1,-1,-1,-1,-1,-1,-1,-1,50,-1,-1,-1
7120 DATA BVS,-1,-1,-1,-1,-1,-1,-1,-1,-1,70,-1,-1,-1
7130 DATA CLC,-1,-1,-1,-1,-1,-1,-1,-1,18,-1,-1,-1,-1
7140 DATA CLD,-1,-1,-1,-1,-1,-1,-1,-1,D8,-1,-1,-1,-1
7150 DATA CLI,-1,-1,-1,-1,-1,-1,-1,-1,58,-1,-1,-1,-1
7160 DATA CLV,-1,-1,-1,-1,-1,-1,-1,-1,B8,-1,-1,-1,-1
7170 DATA CMP,-1,C9,C5,D5,-1,CD,DD,D9,-1,-1,C1,D1,-1
7180 DATA CPX,-1,E0,E4,-1,-1,EC,-1,-1,-1,-1,-1,-1,-1
7190 DATA CPY,-1,C0,C4,-1,-1,CC,-1,-1,-1,-1,-1,-1,-1
7200 DATA DEC,-1,-1,C6,D6,-1,CE,DE,-1,-1,-1,-1,-1,-1
7210 DATA DEX,-1,-1,-1,-1,-1,-1,-1,-1,CA,-1,-1,-1,-1
7220 DATA DEY,-1,-1,-1,-1,-1,-1,-1,-1,88,-1,-1,-1,-1
7230 DATA EOR,-1,49,45,55,-1,4D,5D,59,-1,-1,41,51,-1
7240 DATA INC,-1,-1,E6,F6,-1,EE,FE,-1,-1,-1,-1,-1,-1
7250 DATA INX,-1,-1,-1,-1,-1,-1,-1,-1,E8,-1,-1,-1,-1
7260 DATA INY,-1,-1,-1,-1,-1,-1,-1,-1,C8,-1,-1,-1,-1
7270 DATA JMP,-1,-1,-1,-1,-1,4C,-1,-1,-1,-1,-1,-1,6C
7280 DATA JSR,-1,-1,-1,-1,-1,20,-1,-1,-1,-1,-1,-1,-1
7290 DATA LDA,-1,A9,A5,B5,-1,AD,BD,B9,-1,-1,A1,B1,-1
7300 DATA LDX,-1,A2,A6,-1,B6,AE,-1,BE,-1,-1,-1,-1,-1
7310 DATA LDY,-1,A0,A4,B4,-1,AC,BC,-1,-1,-1,-1,-1,-1
7320 DATA LSR,4A,-1,46,56,-1,4E,5E,-1,-1,-1,-1,-1,-1
7330 DATA NOP,-1,-1,-1,-1,-1,-1,-1,-1,EA,-1,-1,-1,-1
7340 DATA ORA,-1,09,05,15,-1,0D,1D,19,-1,-1,01,11,-1
7350 DATA PHA,-1,-1,-1,-1,-1,-1,-1,-1,48,-1,-1,-1,-1
7360 DATA PHP,-1,-1,-1,-1,-1,-1,-1,-1,08,-1,-1,-1,-1
7370 DATA PLA,-1,-1,-1,-1,-1,-1,-1,-1,68,-1,-1,-1,-1
7380 DATA PLP,-1,-1,-1,-1,-1,-1,-1,-1,28,-1,-1,-1,-1
7390 DATA ROL,2A,-1,26,36,-1,2E,3E,-1,-1,-1,-1,-1,-1
7400 DATA ROR,6A,-1,66,76,-1,6E,7E,-1,-1,-1,-1,-1,-1
7410 DATA RTI,-1,-1,-1,-1,-1,-1,-1,-1,40,-1,-1,-1,-1
7420 DATA RTS,-1,-1,-1,-1,-1,-1,-1,-1,60,-1,-1,-1,-1
7430 DATA SBC,-1,E9,E5,F5,-1,ED,FD,F9,-1,-1,E1,F1,-1
7440 DATA SEC,-1,-1,-1,-1,-1,-1,-1,-1,38,-1,-1,-1,-1
7450 DATA SED,-1,-1,-1,-1,-1,-1,-1,-1,F8,-1,-1,-1,-1
7460 DATA SEI,-1,-1,-1,-1,-1,-1,-1,-1,78,-1,-1,-1,-1
7470 DATA STA,-1,-1,85,95,-1,8D,9D,99,-1,-1,81,91,-1
7480 DATA STX,-1,-1,86,-1,96,8E,-1,-1,-1,-1,-1,-1,-1
7490 DATA STY,-1,-1,84,94,-1,8C,-1,-1,-1,-1,-1,-1,-1
7500 DATA TAX,-1,-1,-1,-1,-1,-1,-1,-1,AA,-1,-1,-1,-1
7510 DATA TAY,-1,-1,-1,-1,-1,-1,-1,-1,A8,-1,-1,-1,-1
7520 DATA TSX,-1,-1,-1,-1,-1,-1,-1,-1,BA,-1,-1,-1,-1
7530 DATA TXA,-1,-1,-1,-1,-1,-1,-1,-1,8A,-1,-1,-1,-1
7540 DATA TXS,-1,-1,-1,-1,-1,-1,-1,-1,9A,-1,-1,-1,-1
7550 DATA TYA,-1,-1,-1,-1,-1,-1,-1,-1,98,-1,-1,-1,-1
```

Description of the 6510 assembler and the important variables.

100 - 190 Display title, read source file name into $SN, prompt for assembly listing. Variable DG is set to the device number for listing depending on the answer. The variable PM determines if the listing is wanted or not. Call routine to initialize the variables with GOSUB 5000.

200 - 460 Main loop of the program. Line 210 performs pass 1 as a subroutine (GOSUB 4000). Source program file opened for reading from disk. If listing is not required, display only the line number $ZN (line 250). Variable for printer output, PR$, is constructed. Line 320 checks for legal instructions. Set error flag if illegal instruction and place BRK instruction at that location. Line 350 determines addressing mode (GOSUB 2400).

Determine direction of branch for relative addressing mode. Call subroutine from line 360 to build string for printing the listing (depending on addressing mode and length of instruction). Write generated code to memory from line 370. Increment program counter in line 380. Print listing in lines 400 thru 460. If error is found, increment error counter in line 420. Display complete assembler source statement in line 450.

500 - 520 Handle one-byte instructions. Variable A% is set to the number of bytes and the instruction code is determined by using T%. A negative value indicates that this instruction cannot use this addressing mode. In this case, branch to 1510, to insert a BRK instruction (zero) instead. Otherwise, convert the opcode to hex and place in the print string.

600 - 740 Handle two-byte instructions. Determine opcode in line 610. Place opcode in print string in line 620. Check for immediate addressing, operators < and > and zero-page addressing (denoted by "*"). Determine if operand is number (hex or decimal) in line 660. If not, get value of the label in line 670 (GOSUB 4500). Convert value of operand to hex. Modify the value according to the operators < and > in line 700 and 710. Range check for value greater than 255 in line 720. Insert value in memory and add to the print string.

800 - 890 Handle three-byte instructions similar to two-byte instructions above. Calculate offset and check for legal address range in line 970. If

illegal, display "R" (range) error and set offset to zero. Convert negative values to two's complement in line 980. Insert the value in memory and add to print string.

1000 - 1420 Execution is transferred here when the assembly is done. Display last line of assembly. Prompt user to save generated code to disk. If yes, setup filename, starting and ending addresses call operating system SAVE routine with SYS. Display range and length of the generated code. Prompt for symbol table display. Sort into alphabetical sequence in lines 1200-1400.

The following are the subroutines which are called from the main routine and perform such operations as number conversion.

1500 - 1520 Output one or two zero bytes if an error was detected during the assembly.

1600 - 1640 Determine if first field is a mnemonic for an instruction or a label. If it is an instruction, assign to variable I the index of that instruction in the assembler's internal tables.

2000 - 2300 Read a source program line from disk and separate into line number, label, instruction mnemonic, operand, and comments. The routine at 2300 reads one byte from disk into the variable Z$. Flag FF% is set if the byte is zero (end-of-line marker). The first two bytes, which contain the link address, are not used. If both are zero, however, the end of the program has been reached and ".EN" in indicated. Otherwise, the line number is obtained from the next two bytes. Find next field by searching for first blank or the end-of-line. If a semicolon is found, the text following is assigned to the variable as comments. Otherwise, the variable ZN$ contains the line number, LN$ contains the label name, X$ contains the instruction mnemonic, Y$ contains the operands, and RM$ contains the comments.

2400 - 2460 Determines the addressing mode of an instruction. Check for characters "(", ")", "," and "X" and "Y". Immediate addressing mode is recognized by "#", and zero-page addressing by "*" (variable ZP, line 2510). Addressing mode is indicated by variable T% as value between zero and twelve. A negative value indicates an illegal addressing mode.

2700 - 2820 Handles the pseudo-instructions "=", "=*", and ".BY". Called during pass 1 and is used for such things as label definition.

2900 - 2998 Handles the same instructions as the previous routine, but for pass 2. This routine places the codes for ".BY" commands in memory.

3000 - 3030 Calls the following routines for number conversion and is used to initialize the print string with the address of the program counter.

3100 - 3230 Convert a hex number in A$ to a decimal number in A.

3240 - 3250 Convert a decimal number in A to a hex number in A$. AL% and AH% contain the low and high bytes, respectively.

4000 - 4280 Perform pass 1 of the assembly. Performs label searching and assigning their values. Also displays the line numbers (line 4060). A hash-code procedure is used for symbol table to speed searching using variable LB$(). The corresponding hex code is placed in HE$(). The length of each instruction is determined from the addressing mode, so that the labels can be assigned the correct values. Check for duplicate labels. Increment the program counter after the determining the address mode T% using the field L%() with the corresponding length of each address mode.

4500 - 4650 Called during pass 2 to determine the value of the label passed in SL$. If the label is not found, an error flag is set, otherwise the hex value is returned in HE$.

5000 - 5070 Initialize all variables from the following DATA statements.

6000 - 7550 DATA statements for the converting from decimal to hex, instruction lengths for different addressing modes, instruction mnemonics and corresponding operation codes and allowable addressing modes.

The following describe the usage of the major variables of the assembler.

SN$	Contains the name of the source program (without suffix ".SRC"). The machine code produced is saved under the same name, with the suffix ".OBJ".
DD$	Contains the drive number.
PG	Contains device number of the output device for the listing; 3 = screen, 4 = printer.
PM	Flag for ignoring printer output (=1).
A	actual address value
AD	immediate program counter during the assembly
ZN$	line number being processed
LN$	label name
X$	instruction mnemonic
Y$	operand
RM$	comments
T%	address mode (zero to twelve)
OF	offset for storage of generated code (0=not used)
A%	length of instruction
A$	hex representation of the actual address A
SL$	label to search for. Must contain the name of the label being searched for when calling 4500.
HE$	hex value of the label
LO	constant 255
HI	constant 256
DF	address offset (difference) for relative addressing
BS%	error counter
MX	number of labels per line for output of symbol table
HI$	"greater" label name for sorting

PR$	string for output of a print line in the listing
MN$	mnemonic
Z$	character from disk
NN%	number of mnemonics (op codes)
X%	ASCII code
ZP	flag for zero-page addressing
HA	value of a label (during pass 1)
F%, FF%	error flags
HC, HC%	hash code
FL$(3)	error codes
LB$(349)	table of labels
HE$(349)	table of corresponding values for labels (in hex code)
T%(55,12)	table of opcodes and address modes. The first index is the instruction word, the second index is the addressing mode.
MN$(55)	table of instruction words in alphabetical order.

6. A Single-Step Simulator for the 6510

If you are still unclear as to how certain machine language instructions work, here's a tool that lets you observe the see the results of each instruction right on the screen. The tool is called a SIMULATOR. As the name implies, it simulates the operation of the 6510 microprocessor. When you RUN the SIMULATOR, it displays the actions and results of an instruction as if that instruction were really being executed.

The SIMULATOR displays the following screen:

```
 PC     AC XR YR SR SP  NV-BDIZC
0000    00 00 00 20 FF  00100000
```

Here are the abbreviation used in the display:

PC	program counter
AC	accumulator
XR	X register
YR	Y register
SR	status register
SP	stack pointer
N	negative flag
V	overflow flag
B	break flag
D	decimal flag
I	interrupt flag
Z	zero flag
C	carry flag

Beneath the abbreviations are the contents of each register. You can change the contents of any register or flag from the keyboard. To change the contents, press the appropriate letter as outlined below. If you press the letter of a flag, then that flag in "inverted". If you press the letter of a register, the screen prompts you for the change. Key in the new value using a legal hexadecimal value and press the <RETURN> key. The new value replaces the old and the display is updated with the new contents. Below is a description of the keys and their respective contents:

P Displays the current contents of the program counter. After changing it, the new value is displayed and the instruction located at this new address is disassembled and also displayed.

A The contents of the accumulator are displayed. You can alter the contents by keying in the new value. After pressing <RETURN>, the new value appears in the register display.

X The contents of the X-register are displayed. You can alter the contents by keying in the new value. After pressing <RETURN>, the new value appears in the register display.

Y The contents of the Y-register are displayed. You can alter the contents by keying in the new value. After pressing <RETURN>, the new value appears in the register display.

S The contents of the stack pointer are displayed. You can alter the contents by keying in the new value. After pressing <RETURN>, the new value of the stack pointer appears in the register display.

The status register SR cannot be changed directly. Instead, you have to change the individual flags which comprise the status register. If a flag is changed, the value of the status register in the display is automatically changed as well.

N By pressing **N**, the value of the Negative flag is inverted: 1 becomes 0 and vice versa. At the same time, the contents of the status register are changed correspondingly, as already mentioned.

V By pressing **V**, the value of the oVerflow flag is inverted as above.

B By pressing B, the value of the Break flag is inverted as above.

D By pressing **D**, the value of the Decimal flag is inverted as above.

I By pressing **I**, the value of the Interrupt flag is inverted as above.

Z By pressing Z, the value of the Zero flag is inverted as above.

C By pressing **C**, the value of the Carry flag is inverted as above.

The most important function of the simulator is performed by pressing the space bar. By pressing the space bar, the machine language instruction pointed to by the program counter is executed. As the name simulator implies, this instruction is not directly executed by the processor. Instead it is simulated by the program. The register contents and flags are altered just as they would be if the microprocessor had executed the instruction. After pressing the space bar, the new contents of the registers and flags are displayed; the next instruction to be executed is disassembled and displayed; the new value of the program counter is displayed.

Below is an example, simulating the execution of a routine contained in the operating system. First set the program counter to $A81D by pressing **P** and entering A81D as the new contents of the program counter. The following is displayed:

```
 PC    AC XR YR SR SP  NV-BDIZC
A81D   00 00 00 20 FF  00100000

A81D 38       SEC
```

Press the space bar to simulate the execution of this instruction. The result appears below:

```
 PC    AC XR YR SR SP  NV-BDIZC
A81E   00 00 00 21 FF  00100001

A81E A5 2B    LDA $2B
```

After the instruction is executed, the carry flag is set. The value of the status register is automatically changed to $21. The program counter is incremented by one to $A81E.

This location contains an LDA instruction. Press the space bar to execute this instruction. Here's what you'll see on the screen:

```
 PC    AC XR YR SR SP  NV-BDIZC
A820   01 00 00 21 FF  00010001

A820 E9 01     SBC #$01
```

The accumulator has been loaded with the contents of memory location $2B, which contains the value 1. Notice that the N and Z flags remain clear because the value loaded was neither zero nor negative. The program counter now stands at $A820, two bytes further. The instruction at this location is SBC #$01 - subtract $01 from the contents of the accumulator. Press the space bar again to see the simulated results of the SBC instruction:

```
 PC    AC XR YR SR SP  NV-BVIZC
A822   00 00 00 23 FF  00100011

A822 A4 2C     LDY $2C
```

After the value $01 is subtracted from the contents of the the accumulator (also 1), the result appears in the accumulator. Something happened to the flags. The zero flag is set, indicating that the result of the operation of is zero. The carry flag is also set. This tells us that underflow did not occur during the subtraction. The next instruction at address $A822 is LDY $2C. Press the space bar to get the following display:

```
 PC    AC XR YR SR SP  NV-BDIZC
A824   00 00 08 21 FF  00100001

A824 B0 01     BCS $A827
```

The Y-register contains $08 and the zero flag is cleared. The instruction at address $A824 is a conditional branch. Can you tell beforehand if this branch will be executed? The branch will take place if the carry flag is set. Since the carry flag is set, the branch will take place. Confirm this by pressing the space bar:

```
 PC    AC XR YR SR SP  NV-BDIZC
A827   00 00 08 21 FF  00100001

A827 85 41     STA $41
```

The program counter is now pointing to $A827, not $A826 has the carry flag been clear. Notice that the flags are not changed by the branch instruction. The next instruction stores the contents of the accumulator in memory location $41. Press the space bar again:

```
 PC    AC XR YR SR SP  NV-BDIZC
A829   00 00 08 21 FF  00100001

A829 84 42     STY $42
```

The STA instruction does not change any of the flags. The next instruction, STY $42, also has no affect on the flags. Press the space bar:

```
 PC    AC XR YR SR SP  NV-BDIZC
A82B   00 00 08 21 FF  00100001

A82B 60        RTS
```

The next instruction is an RTS. You can stop the simulator

here. The great advantage of a simulator is that you can see exactly what each instruction does at your own pace. You can change the contents of the registers and flags at your discretion before the execution of each instruction to see how the processor reacts. You can also set the program counter back to the same instruction after its execution and re-execute it again with different registers or flag values. It becomes a great learning tool.

A simulator also allows you to advance the program counter to the next instruction without executing the previous one. You can do this by pressing the "cursor down" key. For example, if you come to a instruction such as STA or INC which overwrites important operating system areas of memory, you risk **crashing** your computer.

For this reason, instructions affecting memory are normally not executed. If these types of instructions are necessary to test your program correctly, (for example if your program depends on the contents of a specific memory location), then you can specify that the program actually execute such commands. To do this, press the E key. The prompt **ACTUAL SIMULATION? Y** appears on the screen. If you press <RETURN>, then all instructions which write to memory are actually executed. If you respond with **N**(o) instead of **Y**(es), you can turn this option off.

The simulator also allows you to view and alter the contents of memory location. To do this, press the M key. The prompt **ADDRESS ?****** appears on the screen. Enter the desired memory location and press <RETURN>. The current contents of that location are displayed on the screen. You can press <RETURN> to leave the contents unaltered, or key in a new value to change the contents. Changes are accepted only if **ACTUAL SIMULATION** was previously selected with **E.**

The next example describes the operation of the stack. The BRK instruction is used to illustrate the stack operation. Start the simulator by typing **RUN.** Enter **E** to select actual simulation mode, and set the program counter to $0002. Next change the contents of memory location $0002 to $00. $00 is the instruction code for the BRK instruction. Everytime a BRK instruction is executed, the simulator's B flag is set. The following appears on the screen:

```
 PC     AC XR YR SR SP  NV-BDIZC
 0002   00 00 00 20 FF  00100000

 0002 00        BRK
```

To better illustrate the stack operations, place unique values into the accumulator, X and Y registers. You can do this by press the A, X and **Y** keys and typing in new values for the coresponding registers. We have altered the contents of the registers to the values displayed on the next page:

```
 PC     AC XR YR SR SP  NV-BDIZC
0002    22 44 88 20 FF  00100000

0002 00        BRK
```

If there is no BRK instruction at address $0002, then press **M** and enter the address $0002. The contents of memory location 2 appears. Alter the contents to $00 (the operation code for the BRK instruction). Now the BRK instruction is displayed on the screen as shown above. Press the space bar and observe the display:

```
 PC     AC XR YR SR SP  NV-BDIZC
FF48    22 44 88 34 FC  00110100

FF48 48        PHA
```

When a BRK instruction is encountered, the processor takes several actions:

1) The B and I flags are set.

2) The contents of the program counter (two bytes) and the status register are saved onto the stack.

3) The stack pointer is decremented by three, in this case from $FF to $FC.

4) The program counter is loaded with the contents of addresses $FFFE and $FFFF (which contains $FF48). $FFEE and $FFFF contain the BRK vector which is the address of a routine which always handles a BRK interrupt.

The instruction at this location is PHA. This instruction places the contents of the accumulator onto the stack. Press the space bar again. You will see this:

```
 PC     AC XR YR SR SP  NV-BDIZC
FF49    22 44 88 34 FB  00110100

FF49 8A        TXA
```

The contents of the accumulator is placed on the stack and the stack pointer is automatitcally decremented. Next the contents of the X-register is copied to the accumulator with the TXA instruction. Press the space bar again.

```
 PC     AC XR YR SR SP  NV-BDIZC
FF4A    44 44 88 34 FB  00110100

FF4A 48        PHA
```

The flags are not changed because the value in the X-register is neither zero nor negative. The PHA instruction pushes the contents of the accumulator on the stack again. Press the space bar once more.

```
 PC     AC XR YR SR SP  NV-BDIZC
FF4B    44 44 88 34 FA  00110100

FF4B 98        TYA
```

Notice that stack pointer is again decremented. Now the contents of the Y-register is placed in the accumulator with the TYA instruction. This time, however, the N flag is set because the value in the Y register is negative (greater than $7F). This is displayed:

```
 PC     AC XR YR SR SP  NV-BDIZC
FF4C    88 44 88 B4 FA  10110100

FF4C 48        PHA
```

The PHA instruction pushes the contents of the accumulator onto the stack again. Now here's a new instruction.

```
  PC    AC XR YR SR SP  NV-BDIZC
 FF4D   88 44 88 B4 F9  10110100

 FF4D BA        TSX
```

The TSX instruction transfers the contents of the status register to the X-register.

Notice that you have saved all of the registers onto the stack in this order: Program Counter and Status register (saved by BRK), Accumulator, X-register and Y-register.

Now let's simulate the instructions at a different part of the operating system. These instructions restore the registers that we just saved so we can further see the operation of the stack.

Before simulating these instructions, set the register values to zero. Then you can observe as the values change to see how the register contents are restored. You can do this by altering the **A**, **X** and **Y** registers to zero.

Next set the program counter to $EA81. The display should look like this:

```
  PC    AC XR YR SR SP  NV-BDIZC
 EA81   00 00 00 B4 F9  10110100

 EA81 68        PLA
```

The machine language routine at $EA81 restores all of the registers and continues execution at the point just before the BRK interrupt occurred.

When the PLA instruction is executed, the data at the top of the stack is placed into the accumulator. The data is $88, which is the original contents of the Y-register above.

```
  PC    AC XR YR SR SP  NV-BDIZC
 EA82   88 00 00 B4 FA  10110100

 EA82 A8        TAY
```

This instruction copies the value in the accumulator to the Y-register:

```
  PC    AC XR YR SR SP  NV-BDIZC
 EA83   88 00 88 B4 FA  10110100

 EA83 68        PLA
```

Now pull the next value from the stack into the accumulator with the PLA instruction and transfer it to the X-register. Press the space bar to see the results:

```
  PC    AC XR YR SR SP  NV-BDIZC
 EA84   44 00 88 34 FB  00110100

 EA84 AA        TAX
```

Notice that each time a value is taken off the stack, the stack pointer is incremented by one. Press the space bar again:

```
  PC     AC XR YR SR SP  NV-BDIZC
 EA85    44 44 88 34 FB  00110100

 EA85 68        PLA
```

The original contents of the accumulator are now pulled from the stack. Press the space bar. The next display looks like this:

```
  PC     AC XR YR SR SP  NV-BDIZC
 EA86    22 44 88 34 FC  00110100

 EA86 40        RTI
```

All of the registers have been restored and the stack pointer again points to the value to which it pointed after the BRK instruction. When using the stack, the important thing to keep in mind is to pull the values off of the stack in the reverse order that you pushed them on. The "last in--first out" principle characterizes this procedure.

Now we can execute the RTI instruction which returns us to the original interrupted program.

```
  PC     AC XR YR SR SP  NV-BDIZC
 0005    22 44 88 20 FF  00010000

 0005 91 B3     STA ($B3),Y
```

The status register is returned to its original value and

the program counter points to the instruction after the BRK instruction.

The simulator is the ideal tool for testing your programs. Here you can see, step by step, if the processor really does what you had intended. Debugging, always a tricky procedure, is much easier with the simulator. Beginners, who are not be acquainted with all of the addressing modes or who may have problems understanding the flag settings, find the simulator especially helpful. The listing of the simulator program appears on the next pages. Following the listing is a short description of the individual routines and the variables used by the program.

```
100 PRINT"{CLR}{WHT}{C/DN}         6510 SINGLE-STEP SIMULATOR"
110 PRINT"          ----------------------------"
120 PRINT"      ┌─────┬────────────────────┬─────────┐"
130 PRINT"      | PC  | AC XR YR SR SP    |NV-BDIZC |"
140 PRINT"      |     |                    |         |"
150 PRINT"      └─────┴────────────────────┴─────────┘"
160 FF=255:HI=256:UL=2↑16:SC=2↑15-1:SP=FF
170 DIM MN$(FF),OP(FF),AD(FF),SP(FF),H$(15)
180 FORJ=0TO15:READH$(J):NEXT
190 FORJ=0TOFF:READMN$(J),OP(J),AD(J):NEXT
200 REM DISPLAY REGISTERS
210 PRINT"{HOME}{C/DN}{C/DN}{C/DN}{C/DN}{C/DN}{C/RT}{C/RT}{C/RT}{C/RT}
{C/RT}";
215 IFPC>=ULTHENPC=PC-UL
220 A=PC:GOSUB2290:PRINT"{C/RT}{C/RT}";
230 A=AC:GOSUB2320:PRINT"{C/RT}";
240 A=XR:GOSUB2320:PRINT"{C/RT}";
250 A=YR:GOSUB2320:PRINT"{C/RT}";
255 GOSUB900:REM SR
260 A=SR:GOSUB2320:PRINT"{C/RT}";
270 A=SP:GOSUB2320:PRINT"{C/RT}{C/RT}";
280 PRINTCHR$(48+N);
290 PRINTCHR$(48+V);
300 PRINT"1";
310 PRINTCHR$(48+B);
320 PRINTCHR$(48+D);
330 PRINTCHR$(48+I);
340 PRINTCHR$(48+Z);
350 PRINTCHR$(48+C)
360 PRINT"{C/DN}{C/DN}{C/DN}{C/DN}{C/DN}                    {C/LF}{C/LF}
{C/LF}{C/LF}{C/LF}{C/LF}{C/LF}{C/LF}{C/LF}{C/LF}{C/LF}{C/LF}{C/LF}{C/LF}
{C/LF}{C/LF}{C/LF}{C/LF}";
400 GETT$:IFT$=""THEN400
405 IF T$=" "THEN1100:REM SIMULATION
410 IFT$="P"THENPRINT"PC  ";:A=PC:GOSUB2290:INPUT"{C/LF}{C/LF}{C/LF}
{C/LF}{C/LF}{C/LF}";A$:GOSUB2380:PC=A
411 IFT$="F"THEN1000
420 IFT$="A"THENT$="AC":A=AC:GOSUB540:AC=A:GOTO200
430 IFT$="X"THENT$="XR":A=XR:GOSUB540:XR=A:GOTO200
440 IFT$="Y"THENT$="YR":A=YR:GOSUB540:YR=A:GOTO200
450 IFT$="S"THENT$="SP":A=SP:GOSUB540:SP=A:GOTO200
460 IFT$="N"THENN=1-N:GOTO200
470 IFT$="V"THENV=1-V:GOTO200
480 IFT$="B"THENB=1-B:GOTO200
490 IFT$="D"THEND=1-D:GOTO200
500 IFT$="I"THENI=1-I:GOTO200
510 IFT$="Z"THENZ=1-Z:GOTO200
520 IFT$="C"THENC=1-C:GOTO200
525 IFT$="{C/DN}"THENS=P:E=P:PC=P:GOTO1010
527 IFT$="M"THEN3000
528 IFT$="E"THEN3100
530 GOTO400
540 PRINTT$"  ";:GOSUB2320:INPUT"{C/LF}{C/LF}{C/LF}{C/LF}";A$
:GOTO2380
900 SR=N*128+V*64+32+B*16+D*8+I*4+Z*2+C:RETURN
910 N=SGN(SRAND128):V=SGN(SRAND64)::B=SGN(SRAND16):D=SGN(SRAND8)
920 I=SGN(SRAND4):Z=SGN(SRAND2):C=SRAND1:RETURN
980 N=SGN(ACAND128):Z=1-SGN(AC):REM FLAGS
```

```
990 PC=PC+1+L
1000 S=PC:E=PC
1010 PRINT"{HOME}{C/DN}{C/DN}{C/DN}{C/DN}{C/DN}{C/DN}{C/DN}{C/DN}"
:GOSUB2040:GOTO200
1100 A=OP(PEEK(PC)):L=0:IFA=0THEN990
1110 ONAGOTO1200,1210,1220,1230,1240,1250,1260,1270,1280,1290,1300,
1310,1320,1330
1115 A=A-14
1120 ONAGOTO1340,1350,1360,1370,1380,1390,1400,1410,1420,1430,1440,
1450,1460,1470
1125 A=A-14
1130 ONAGOTO1480,1490,1500,1510,1520,1530,1540,1550,1560,1570,1580,
1590,1600,1610
1135 A=A-14
1140 ONAGOTO1620,1630,1640,1650,1660,1670,1680,1690,1700,1710,1720,
1730,1740,1750
1150 GOTO200
1200 IFDTHEN1205:REM ADC
1201 GOSUB1900:V=1-SGN(ACAND128):AC=AC+OP+C:C=-(AC>FF)
1202 AC=ACANDFF:N=SGN(ACAND128):V=VANDN:GOTO980
1205 GOSUB1900:AC=VAL(H$(AC/16)+H$(ACAND15)):OP=VAL(H$(OP/16)+H$
(OPAND15))
1206 AC=AC+OP+C:C=-(AC>99):IFAC>99THENAC=AC-100
1207 A$=MID$(STR$(AC),2):GOSUB2390:AC=A:GOTO980
1210 REM AND
1211 GOSUB1900:AC=ACANDOP:GOTO980
1220 GOSUB1900:A=OP*2:C=-(A>FF):A=AANDFF:GOSUB1850
1221 IFAD(PEEK(PC))=4THENAC=AC*2:C=-(AC>FF):AC=ACANDFF:GOTO980
1223 N=SGN(OPANDFF):Z=1-SGN(OP):GOTO990
1230 REM BCC
1240 REM BCS
1241 FL=C:GOTO1800
1250 REM BEQ
1251 FL=Z:GOTO1800
1260 REM BIT
1261 GOSUB1900:N=SGN(OPAND128):V=SGN(OPAND64):Z=1-SGN(OPANDAC)
:GOTO990
1270 REM BMI
1271 FL=N:GOTO1800
1280 REM BNE
1281 FL=1-Z:GOTO1800
1290 REM BPL
1300 REM BRK
1301 PC=PC+2:IFPC>=ULTHENPC=PC-2
1302 PH=INT(PC/HI):PL=PC-PH*HI:SP(SP)=PH:SP=SP-1ANDFF:SP(SP)=PL
:SP=SP-1ANDFF
1303 B=1:I=1:GOSUB900:SP(SP)=SR:SP=SP-1ANDFF:PC=PEEK(65534)
+HI*PEEK(65535)
1304 GOTO1000
1310 REM BVC
1311 FL=1-V:GOTO1800
1320 REM BVS
1321 FL=V:GOTO1800
1330 REM CLC
1331 C=0:GOTO1800
1340 REM CLD
1341 D=0:GOTO990
1350 REM CLI
1351 I=0:GOTO990
1360 REM CLV
1361 V=0:GOTO990
1370 REM CMP
```

```
1371 GOSUB1900:A=AC-OP
1372 N=SGN(AAND128):Z=-(A=0):C=-(A>=0):GOTO990
1380 REM CPX
1381 GOSUB1900:A=XR-OP:GOTO1372
1390 REM CPY
1391 GOSUB1900:A=YR-OP:GOTO1372
1400 REM DEC
1401 GOSUB1900:A=OP-1ANDFF:GOSUB1850
1402 GOTO1442
1410 REM DEX
1411 XR=(XR-1)ANDFF:GOTO1452
1420 REM DEY
1421 YR=(YR-1)ANDFF:GOTO1462
1430 REM EOR
1431 GOSUB1900:A=0:FORJ=7TOOSTEP-1:EX=2↑J:A=2*A-((OPANDEX)<>
 (ACANDEX)):NEXT
1432 AC=A:GOTO980
1440 REM INC
1441 GOSUB1900:A=OP+1ANDFF:GOSUB1850
1442 N=SGN(AAND128):Z=1-SGN(A):GOTO990
1450 REM INX
1451 XR=(XR+1)ANDFF
1452 Z=1-SGN(XR):N=SGN(XRAND128):GOTO990
1460 REM INY
1461 YR=(YR+1)ANDFF
1462 Z=1-SGN(YR):N=SGN(YRAND128):GOTO990
1470 REM JMP
1471 GOSUB1900:PC=AD:GOTO1000
1480 REM JSR
1481 A=PC+2:PH=INT(A/HI):PL=A-PH*HI:SP(SP)=PH:SP=SP-1ANDFF:SP(SP)=PL
 :SP=SP-1ANDFF
1482 PC=PEEK(PC+1)+PEEK(PC+2)*HI:GOTO1000
1490 REM LDA
1491 GOSUB1900:AC=OP:GOTO980
1500 REM LDX
1501 GOSUB1900:XR=OP:GOTO1452
1510 REM LDY
1511 GOSUB1900:YR=OP:GOTO1462
1520 REM LSR
1521 IFAD(PEEK(PC))<>4THEN1524
1522 AC=AC/2
1523 C=-(AC<>INT(AC)):AC=ACANDFF:GOTO980
1524 GOSUB1900:A=OP/2:C=-(A<>INT(A)):A=AANDFF:GOSUB1850
1525 GOTO1442
1530 REM NOP
1531 GOTO990
1540 REM ORA
1541 GOSUB1900:AC=ACOROP:GOTO980
1550 REM PHA
1551 SP(SP)=AC:SP=SP-1ANDFF:GOTO990
1560 REM PHP
1561 GOSUB900:SP(SP)=SR:SP=SP-1ANDFF:GOTO990
1570 REM PLA
1571 SP=(SP+1)ANDFF:AC=SP(SP):GOTO980:REM SET FLAGS
1580 REM PLP
1581 SP=(SP+1)ANDFF:SR=SP(SP):GOSUB910:GOTO990
1590 REM ROL
1591 IFAD(PEEK(PC))=4THENAC=AC*2+C:GOTO1522
1592 GOSUB1900:A=OP*2+C:C=-(A>FF)
```

```
1593 A=AANDFF:GOSUB1850
1594 GOTO1442
1600 REM ROR
1601 IFAD(PEEK(PC))=4THENAC=AC/2+128*C:GOTO1523
1602 GOSUB1900:A=OP/2+128*C:C=-(A<>INT(A)):GOTO1593
1610 REM RTI
1611 SP=SP+1ANDFF:SR=SP(SP):GOSUB910:GOTO1621
1620 REM RTS
1621 SP=SP+1ANDFF:A=SP(SP):SP=SP+1ANDFF:PC=A+SP(SP)*HI:GOTO990
1630 IFDTHEN1635:  REM SBC
1631 GOSUB1900:V=SGN(ACAND128):AC=AC-OP-1+C:C=-(AC>=0)
1632 AC=ACANDFF:N=SGN(ACAND128):V=VAND1-N:GOTO980
1635 GOSUB1900:AC=VAL(H$(AC/16)+H$(ACAND15)):OP=VAL(H$(OP/16)+H$
(OPAND15))
1636 AC=AC-OP+C-1:C=-(AC>=0):IFAC<0THENAC=AC+100
1637 A$=MID$(STR$(AC),2):GOSUB2390:AC=A:GOTO980
1640 REM SEC
1641 C=1:GOTO990
1650 REM SED
1651 D=1:GOTO990
1660 REM SEI
1661 I=1:GOTO990
1670 REM STA
1671 GOSUB1900:A=AC:GOSUB1850
1672 GOTO990
1680 REM STX
1681 GOSUB1900:A=XR:GOSUB1850
1682 GOTO990
1690 REM STY
1691 GOSUB1900:A=YR:GOSUB1850
1692 GOTO990
1700 REM TAX
1701 XR=AC:GOTO1452
1710 REM TAY
1711 YR=AC:GOTO1462
1720 REM TSX
1721 XR=SP:GOTO1452
1730 REM TXA
1731 AC=XR:GOTO980
1740 REM TXS
1741 SP=XR:GOTO990
1750 REM TYA
1751 AC=YR:GOTO980
1800 REM BRANCH COMMANDS
1810 IFFL=0THENL=1:GOTO990
1820 GOSUB1985:GOTO1000
1850 REM POKE
1870 IFAD<HIORAD>HI+FFTHEN1880
1875 SP(AD-HI)=A:RETURN
1880 IFESTHENPOKEAD,A
1885 RETURN
1900 REM GET OPERAND
1910 A=AD(PEEK(PC))
1920 ONAGOSUB1930,1935,1940,1945,1950,1955,1960,1965,1970,1975,
1980,1985,1990
1925 IFAD<HIORAD>HI+FFTHENRETURN
1927 OP=SP(AD-HI):RETURN
1930 AD=0:RETURN:REM IMPLIED
1935 AD=PC+1:OP=PEEK(AD):L=1:RETURN:REM #
1940 AD=PEEK(PC+1):OP=PEEK(AD):L=1:RETURN:REM ZERO-PAGE
```

```
1945 AD=0:RETURN:REM A
1950 AD=PEEK(PC+1)+HI*PEEK(PC+2):OP=PEEK(AD):L=2:RETURN
1955 AD=PEEK(PC+1)+XRANDFF:OP=PEEK(AD):L=1:RETURN
1960 AD=PEEK(PC+1)+YRANDFF:OP=PEEK(AD):L=1:RETURN
1965 AD=PEEK(PC+1)+HI*PEEK(PC+2)+XR:OP=PEEK(AD):L=2:RETURN
1970 AD=PEEK(PC+1)+HI*PEEK(PC+2)+YR:OP=PEEK(AD):L=2:RETURN
1975 AD=PEEK(PEEK(PC+1))+HI*PEEK(PEEK(PC+1)+1ANDFF)+YR:OP=PEEK(AD)
 :L=1:RETURN
1980 AD=PEEK(PC+1)+XRANDFF:AD=PEEK(AD)+HI*PEEK(AD+1):OP=PEEK(AD)
 :L=1:RETURN
1985 A=PEEK(PC+1):A=A+HI*(A>127)+2+PC
1986 PC=INT(A/HI)*HI+((A+(A>SC)*UL)ANDFF):RETURN:REM RELATIVE
1990 AD=PEEK(PC+1)+HI*PEEK(PC+2):AD=PEEK(AD)+HI*PEEK(AD+1):OP=PEEK
 (AD):RETURN
2040 FORP=STOE:PRINT" ";
2050 A=P:GOSUB2290:REM ADDRESS
2060 PRINT" ";:A=PEEK(P):GOSUB2320:PRINT" ";:J=PEEK(P):OP=AD(J)
2070 ONOPGOSUB2350,2360,2360,2350,2370,2360,2360,2370,2370,2360,2360,
 2360,2370
2080 PRINT" ";MN$(J)" ";
2090 ONOPGOSUB2110,2120,2130,2140,2150,2160,2170,2180,2190,2200,2210,
 2220,2240
2100 PRINT"            ":NEXTP
2105 IFP>=ULTHENP=P-UL
2110 RETURN
2120 PRINT"#";:GOSUB2330:P=P+1:RETURN
2130 GOSUB2330:P=P+1:RETURN
2140 PRINT" A";:RETURN
2150 GOSUB2260:P=P+2:RETURN
2160 GOSUB2330:P=P+1:PRINT",X";:RETURN
2170 GOSUB2330:P=P+2:PRINT",Y";:RETURN
2180 GOSUB2260:P=P+2:PRINT",X";:RETURN
2190 GOSUB2260:P=P+2:PRINT",Y";:RETURN
2200 PRINT"(";:GOSUB2330:P=P+1:PRINT"),Y";:RETURN
2210 PRINT"(";:GOSUB2330:P=P+1:PRINT",X)";:RETURN
2220 A=PEEK(P+1):A=A+HI*(A>127)+2+P
2230 A=INT(A/HI)*HI+((A+(A>SC)*UL)ANDFF):PRINT"$";:GOSUB2290
 :P=P+1:RETURN
2240 PRINT"(";:GOSUB2260
2250 PRINT")";:P=P+2:RETURN
2260 PRINT"$";
2270 A=PEEK(P+1)+HI*PEEK(P+2)
2280 REM HEX ADDRESS A
2290 HB=INT(A/HI):A=A-HI*HB
2300 PRINTH$(HB/16)H$(HBAND15);
2310 REM HEX BYTE A
2320 PRINTH$(A/16)H$(AAND15);:RETURN
2330 PRINT"$";
2340 A=PEEK(P+1):GOTO2320
2350 PRINT"      ";:RETURN
2360 GOSUB2340:PRINT"   ";:RETURN
2370 GOSUB2340:PRINT" ";:A=PEEK(P+2):GOTO2320
2380 IFASC(A$)=42THENEND
2390 A=0:FORJ=1TOLEN(A$):X=ASC(RIGHT$(A$,J))-48:X=X+(X>9)*7:A=A+X*
 (16↑(J-1)):NEXT
2391 RETURN
3000 PRINT:PRINT"{C/DN}{C/DN}":PRINT"ADDRESS:    $****{C/LF}{C/LF}
 {C/LF}{C/LF}{C/LF}{C/LF}";:INPUTA$:GOSUB2380
3010 PRINT"{C/UP}",,:AD=A:OP=PEEK(AD):A=OP:GOSUB2320:INPUT"{C/LF}
 {C/LF}{C/LF}{C/LF}";A$:GOSUB2380
3020 GOSUB1850:PRINT"{C/UP}                                   ":IFAD=PC
 THEN1000
3030 GOTO200
3100 INPUT"ACTUAL SIMULATION   Y{C/LF}{C/LF}{C/LF}";ES$:ES=ES$="Y"
3110 PRINT"{C/UP}                                   ":GOTO200
```

```
10000 DATA 0,1,2,3,4,5,6,7,8,9,A,B,C,D,E,F
10010 DATA"BRK",11,1,"ORA",35,11,"???",0,1
10020 DATA"???",0,1,"???",0,1,"ORA",35,3
10030 DATA"ASL",3,3,"???",0,1,"PHP",37,1
10040 DATA"ORA",35,2,"ASL",3,4,"???",0,1
10050 DATA"???",0,1,"ORA",35,5,"ASL",3,5
10060 DATA"???",0,1,"BPL",10,12,"ORA",35,10
10070 DATA"???",0,1,"???",0,1,"???",0,1
10080 DATA"ORA",35,6,"ASL",3,6,"???",0,1
10090 DATA"CLC",14,1,"ORA",35,9,"???",0,1
10100 DATA"???",0,1,"???",0,1,"ORA",35,8
10110 DATA"ASL",3,8,"???",0,1,"JSR",29,5
10120 DATA"AND",2,11,"???",0,1,"???",0,1
10130 DATA"BIT",7,3,"AND",2,3,"ROL",40,3
10140 DATA"???",0,1,"PLP",39,1,"AND",2,2
10150 DATA"ROL",40,4,"???",0,1,"BIT",7,5
10160 DATA"AND",2,5,"ROL",40,5,"???",0,1
10170 DATA"BMI",8,12,"AND",2,10,"???",0,1
10180 DATA"???",0,1,"???",0,1,"AND",2,6
10190 DATA"ROL",40,6,"???",0,1,"SEC",45,1
10200 DATA"AND",2,9,"???",0,1,"???",0,1
10210 DATA"???",0,1,"AND",2,8,"ROL",40,8
10220 DATA"???",0,1,"RTI",42,1,"EOR",24,11
10230 DATA"???",0,1,"???",0,1,"???",0,1
10240 DATA"EOR",24,3,"LSR",33,3,"???",0,1
10250 DATA"PHA",36,1,"EOR",24,2,"LSR",33,4
10260 DATA"???",0,1,"JMP",28,5,"EOR",24,5
10270 DATA"LSR",33,5,"???",0,1,"BVC",12,12
10280 DATA"EOR",24,10,"???",0,1,"???",0,1
10290 DATA"???",0,1,"EOR",24,6,"LSR",33,6
10300 DATA"???",0,1,"CLI",16,1,"EOR",24,9
10310 DATA"???",0,1,"???",0,1,"???",0,1
10320 DATA"EOR",24,8,"LSR",33,8,"???",0,1
10330 DATA"RTS",43,1,"ADC",1,11,"???",0,1
10340 DATA"???",0,1,"???",0,1,"ADC",1,3
10350 DATA"ROR",41,3,"???",0,1,"PLA",38,1
10360 DATA"ADC",1,2,"ROR",41,4,"???",0,1
10370 DATA"JMP",28,13,"ADC",1,5,"ROR",41,5
10380 DATA"???",0,1,"BVS",13,12,"ADC",1,10
10390 DATA"???",0,1,"???",0,1,"???",0,1
10400 DATA"ADC",1,6,"ROR",41,6,"???",0,1
10410 DATA"SEI",47,1,"ADC",1,9,"???",0,1
10420 DATA"???",0,1,"???",0,1,"ADC",1,8
10430 DATA"ROR",41,8,"???",0,1,"???",0,1
10440 DATA"STA",48,11,"???",0,1,"???",0,1
10450 DATA"STY",50,3,"STA",48,3,"STX",49,3
10460 DATA"???",0,1,"DEY",23,1,"???",0,1
10470 DATA"TXA",54,1,"???",0,1,"STY",50,5
10480 DATA"STA",48,5,"STX",49,5,"???",0,1
10490 DATA"BCC",4,12,"STA",48,10,"???",0,1
10500 DATA"???",0,1,"STY",50,6,"STA",48,6
10510 DATA"STX",49,7,"???",0,1,"TYA",56,1
10520 DATA"STA",48,9,"TXS",55,1,"???",0,1
10530 DATA"???",0,1,"STA",48,8,"???",0,1
10540 DATA"???",0,1,"LDY",32,2,"LDA",30,11
10550 DATA"LDX",31,2,"???",0,1,"LDY",32,3
10560 DATA"LDA",30,3,"LDX",31,3,"???",0,1
10570 DATA"TAY",52,1,"LDA",30,2,"TAX",51,1
```

```
10580 DATA"???",0,1,"LDY",32,5,"LDA",30,5
10590 DATA"LDX",31,5,"???",0,1,"BCS",5,12
10600 DATA"LDA",30,10,"???",0,1,"???",0,1
10610 DATA"LDY",32,6,"LDA",30,6,"LDX",31,7
10620 DATA"???",0,1,"CLV",17,1,"LDA",30,9
10630 DATA"TSX",53,1,"???",0,1,"LDY",32,8
10640 DATA"LDA",30,8,"LDX",31,9,"???",0,1
10650 DATA"CPY",20,2,"CMP",18,11,"???",0,1
10660 DATA"???",0,1,"CPY",20,3,"CMP",18,3
10670 DATA"DEC",21,3,"???",0,1,"INY",27,1
10680 DATA"CMP",18,2,"DEX",22,1,"???",0,1
10690 DATA"CPY",20,5,"CMP",18,5,"DEC",21,5
10700 DATA"???",0,1,"BNE",9,12,"CMP",18,10
10710 DATA"???",0,1,"???",0,1,"???",0,1
10720 DATA"CMP",18,6,"DEC",21,6,"???",0,1
10730 DATA"CLD",15,1,"CMP",18,9,"???",0,1
10740 DATA"???",0,1,"???",0,1,"CMP",18,8
10750 DATA"DEC",21,8,"???",0,1,"CPX",19,2
10760 DATA"SBC",44,1,"???",0,1,"???",0,1
10770 DATA"CPX",19,3,"SBC",44,3,"INC",25,3
10780 DATA"???",0,1,"INX",26,1,"SBC",44,2
10790 DATA"NOP",34,1,"???",0,1,"CPX",19,5
10800 DATA"SBC",44,5,"INC",25,5,"???",0,1
10810 DATA"BEQ",6,12,"SBC",44,10,"???",0,1
10820 DATA"???",0,1,"???",0,1,"SBC",44,6
10830 DATA"INC",25,6,"???",0,1,"SED",46,1
10840 DATA"SBC",44,9,"???",0,1,"???",0,1
10850 DATA"???",0,1,"SBC",44,8,"INC",25,8
10860 DATA"???",0,1
```

Program description for the single-step simulator

100 - 190	Build the register display, initialize variables and fields.
200 - 360	Display the register contents. The contents of the registers are displayed in hexadecimal. The flags are displayed using the CHR$ function by adding the value of the flag (0 or 1) to 48.
400 - 530	The keys are tested. If the space bar is pressed, execution passes to the simulator routine at line 1100. The register commands result in branches to input routines which display the old value and wait for the input of the new value. For the flags, the state is simply reversed. If the "cursor down" key is pressed, the disassembler routine is called and the next instruction is displayed.
900 - 920	Calculate the value of the status register SR based on the individual flags.
980	Set N and Z flags.
990	Increment program counter.
1000 - 1010	Disassemble the next instruction.
1100 - 1150	Perform single-step simulation. The appropriate routine is called depending on the operation code.
1200 - 1751	Simulate routine for all 6510 commands. The routines are alphabetically ordered by mnemonic. The prqogram counter is incremented according to the length of the instruction in line 990. The N and Z flags are set according to the value in the accumulator by a jump to line 980.
1800 - 1820	All branch commands are handled here, after the corresponding flag value is placed in the variable FL.
1850 - 1885	This routine is used to write values in memory. The stack area from $100 to $1FF is handled differently. The POKEs are executed only if actual simulation is desired (variable ES).
1900 - 1990	Get the operands for the commands based on the addressing mode. After calling this routine, the address of the operand is in AD, the value itself in OP.

2040 - 2370 Disassembles then next instruction after each single step. The operand is displayed according to the addressing mode in line 2070. If the memory location does not contain a legal instruction code, three question marks are displayed instead. The following routines carry out the addressed task as well as the conversion from decimal to hex.

3000 - 3030 Displays and changes the memory contents. The changes are allowed only if the actual simulation is selected.

3100 Select the actual simulation parameters.

10000-10860 Contain the instruction mnemonics, operation codes and addressing modes.

Descriptions of the important variables.

FF	constant 255
HI	constant 255
UL	constant 65536
SC	constant 32767
MN$(255)	table of 6510 mnemonics
OP(255)	table with the corresponding operation codes for the single-step simulation
AD(255)	table with the addressing mode for each instruction.
SP(255)	the simulator stack
H$(15)	field with hex digits
PC	program counter
AC	accumulator
XR	X register
YR	Y register
SR	status register
SP	stack pointer
N	negative flag
V	overflow flag
B	break flag
D	decimal flag
I	interrupt flag
Z	zero flag
C	carry flag
T$	pressed key
L	length of operands
ES	flag for actual simulation
OP	operand

7. Machine Language Programming on the Commodore 64

Machine language is particularly well-suited for programming high resolution graphics on the Commodore 64. In this section. We begin by programming graphics in BASIC and then converting the corresponding routines to machine language. By doing this, you will become well acquainted with many machine language programming techniques.

Graphics programming can be done in BASIC only with a confusing set of PEEKs and POKESs. By writing a few machine language routines we can greatly simplify these graphics. You will learn how to combine machine language programs with BASIC programs, thereby taking advantage of the strong points of both languages.

The programming details of the video-controller kernal routines are discussed only as much as necessary to solve our problem. If you want to get a closer look at the hardware and operating system of the Commodore 64, we recommend the book **The Anatomy of the Commodore 64** available from ABACUS Software.

Before you turn to the first example, take a look at how you can use machine language programs from BASIC and how how to pass parameters between the two programs.

The normal way to call a machine language program from BASIC is to use the SYS command to specify the memory location where execution is to begin. SYS assumes that the machine language program is already in memory and then passing control to it. When the machine language program executes an RTS instruction (return from subroutine), execution returns to the BASIC statement following the SYS command.

Some machine language routines require no parameters to be passed to it. A routine for clearing the screen, for example, does not require any parameters.

Other routines require parameters. A routine for plotting a point requires an X and Y coordinate, for example.

How can you pass parameters to machine language routines?

There are several different techniques for passing parameters:

a. Using the pigeon-hole method, you can place the parameters in one or more memory locations previously agreed upon. For our example, one memory location contains the horizontal coordinate and another memory location the vertical coordinate. You can do this from BASIC with two POKE commands. The machine language program can then get the values of the coordinates from the memory locations and process them.

b. Using the register pass area method, you can pass values between the BASIC program and the machine language program. When a SYS command is executed by BASIC, it is possible to transfer specific values through the registers. Because we cannot access the processor registers directly from BASIC, four memory locations are reserved for this purpose. When the SYS instruction is executed, the contents of the following memory locations are copied into the registers before the branch to the routine is made.

```
780  =>  accumulator
781  =>  X register
782  =>  Y register
783  =>  status register
```

To start a machine language routine with a specific value in the accumulator, you would POKE location 780 with the desired value. Addresses 781 and 782 pertain to the X and Y registers. Caution must be exercised in assigning a value to the status register. Take care not to unintentionally set the decimal or interrupt flag since this can lead to complications.

After the machine language routine is finished, the contents of these registers are saved in these same memory locations. So the machine language routine can pass information back to the BASIC program using the same technique. To retrieve a value, the BASIC program merely PEEKs the desired register pass area. Using this method, it is possible to transfer three or possibly four 8-bit values between the BASIC and machine language programs. This should suffice for most applications. If more parameters must be transferred, you must establish memory locations as described above.

c. Using the BASIC interpreter formula evaluation routine, you can pass an almost unlimited number of parameters to the machine language routine. For example, when the interpreter encounters an instruction such as **POKE 780,10**, it uses a built-in ROM routine to evaluate the parameters following the POKE keyword. This routine evaluates not only constants, but complicated expressions as well, such as POKE A+7.5*Z%(INT(SIN(X)*1000)),EXP(X). You can call this ROM routine from your own machine langauge program. Later you will see how to use these routines. For now, use the register pass area to transfer parameters directly via the registers.

Before discussing graphics programming, you should be acquainted with a few principles.

The distinguishing characteristic of high resolution graphics is that you can access each individual pixel on the screen. This is unlike the normal text mode, where you can access only complete characters (8X8 pixels). For normal text there are 25 * 40 characters at your disposal; with high resolution graphics there are eight times as many in each direction, 200 * 320 points.

In normal text mode, each character requires one byte in video RAM. Each screen location can display any of 256 different characters. Normal text mode requires 25 * 40 * 1 = 1000 bytes of memory called video RAM. Video RAM is located beginning at address 1024 thru 2023 ($400 to $7E8). This starting address of the video RAM can be changed in steps of 1 Kbyte ($400, $800, $C000, $1000, etc.) by programming the video controller.

In high resolution graphics mode, each point requires one bit. Each pixel can be either on or off. High resolution graphics requires 200 * 320 * 1 bit = 64000 bits = 8000 bytes of memory. Memory used in this way is often called the bit-mapped area. The starting address of the bit-mapped area is specified by programming the video controller in the Commodore 64.

Before programming the video controller, you have to first decide where the 8K bit-mapped area is to be located. At first, you may be tempted to use 8K storage from the area that BASIC normally uses. But since you are programming in machine language you have other alternatives. The Commodore 64 has a full 64K of RAM, in addition to the ROMS, input and output devices and character ROMS. You can use the RAM that lies "underneath" (in the same address range) the BASIC and kernal ROM. This area is located beginning at address $E000 to $FFFF. Normally you cannot use this area from BASIC because you must first turn off the BASIC interpreter and operating system when accessing these locations.

The video RAM normally used for the text screen is used as color memory when using high resolution graphics. Since the video RAM and bit-mapped areas must be located within the same 16K range ($C000 - $FFFF), you can use the from $C000 to $C3FF for color memory. Since there is only 1K of video RAM available for use as color memory, each byte of video RAM determines the color of the 64 pixels within the field of an 8x8 cells.

Now we present several routines which you can use for programming in high resolution graphics.

The first routine changes the Commodore 64 from text mode to high resolution graphics mode. By using the area bemeath the ROMS for the bit-mapped graphics area, the normal text screen contents are not destroyed. The contents is preserved when we switch from one mode to another. Here's the program in pseudo-BASIC. Of course this BASIC program does not run since we cannot use hexadecimal numbers as constants.

```
100 V = 53428 : REM VIDEO CONTROLLER START ADDRESS
110 V1 = V+17 : REM GRAPHICS-MODE SWITCH ADDRESS
120 V2 = V+24 : REM VIDEO RAM ADDRESS
130 CIA = $DD00 : REM 16K RANGE
140 POKE V1,59
150 POKE V2,8
160 POKE CIA,0
170 END
```

To convert this to machine language, first decide where the machine language program is to be stored. Since the area from $C000 to $C400 is used as color memory, use the area beginning at $C400 for the program. The conversions of these commands to machine language is straight-forward. Remember to RUN the short program UNTOKEN before creating the following assembler source program.

```
100 VIDEO = 53248 ; VIDEO CONTROLLER
110 V1 = 53625 : ADDRESS FOR GRAPHICS MODE
120 V2 = 53272 ; ADDRESS FOR VIDEO RAM ADDRESS
130 CIA = $DD00 ; 16K SELECTION
140 *= $C400 ; START OF OUR ROUTINE
150 LDA #59
160 STA V1
170 LDA #8
180 STA V2
190 LDA #0
200 STA CIA
210 RTS
220 .EN
```

Assembling the above program, gives you this listing:

```
D000                    100 VIDEO   =      53248
D011                    110 V1      =      53265
D018                    120 V2      =      53272
DD00                    130 CIA     =      $DD00
                        140         *=     $C400
C400  A9 3B             150 ON      LDA    #59
C402  8D 11 D0          160         STA    V1
C405  A9 08             170         LDA    #8
C407  8D 18 D0          180         STA    V2
C40A  A9 00             190         LDA    #0
C40C  8D 00 DD          200         STA    CIA
C40F  60                210         RTS
                        220         .EN
```

Now let's write a routine which switches the Commodore 64 back to normal text mode. You do this by loading the video controller registers with their original values. For the sake of simplicity, append this routine to the previous one.

```
100 VIDEO = 53248 ; VIDEO CONTROLLER
110 V1 = 53625 : ADDRESS FOR GRAPHICS MODE
120 V2 = 53272 ; ADDRESS FOR VIDEO RAM ADDRESS
130 CIA = $DD00 ; 16K SELECTION
140 *= $C400 ; START OF OUR ROUTINE
150 ON LDA #59
160 STA V1
170 LDA #8
180 STA V2
190 LDA #0
200 STA CIA
210 RTS
220 ; TURN OFF
230 OFF LDA #27
240 LDA V1
250 LDA #21
260 STA V2
270 LDA #3
280 STA CIA
290 RTS
300 .EN
```

After assembling this program, you should display the symbol table. The symbols ON and OFF have been defined, even though they are not referred to in the program? We have done this because these addresses are used later for the calls via the SYS instruction.

```
D000                 100 VIDEO  =      53248
D011                 110 V1     =      53265
D018                 120 V2     =      53272
DD00                 130 CIA    =      $DD00
                     140        *=     $C400
C400  A9 3B          150 ON     LDA    #59
C402  8D 11 D0       160        STA    V1
C405  A9 08          170        LDA    #8
C407  8D 18 D0       180        STA    V2
C40A  A9 00          190        LDA    #0
C40C  8D 00 DD       200        STA    CIA
C40F  60             210        RTS
C410                 220                      ; TURN OFF
C410  A9 1B          230 OFF    LDA    #27
C412  8D 11 D0       240        STA    V1
C415  A9 15          250        LDA    #21
C417  8D 18 D0       260        STA    V2
C41A  A9 03          270        LDA    #3
C41C  8D 00 DD       280        STA    CIA
C41F  60             290        RTS
                     300        .EN

C400 / C420 / 0020
SOURCE FILE IS EXAMPLE.SRC
 0  ERRORS

OFF    C410     CIA   DD00    ON   C400
VIDEO  D000     V1    D011    V2   D018
```

Before you test these routines, convert the starting addresses ON and OFF into decimal: $C400 is equal to 50176, $C410 is equal to 50192. You can test the routines by using a short BASIC program:

```
100 SYS 50176 : REM GRAPHICS ON
110 GET A$ : IF A$="" THEN 110
120 SYS 50192 : REM GRAPHICS OFF
```

This program switches to the high resolution graphics mode, waits for a key press and then switches back to the normal text mode. Try it!

When you RUN the program, a mixture of colored squares appears on the screen. What you see are the random values that the unused RAM area contains after the computer is turned on. If you press a key, you return to the normal text screen mode.

The next task is to clear the high-resolution graphic screen and color memory. In BASIC you can perform this by using a loop to POKE the bit-mapped graphics area.

To erase all the points in the bit-mapped graphics area, each bit must be set zero. Therefore each byte of the bit-mapped area is also set to zero. The loop must clear the area beginning at address $E000 through $FFFF (actually to $FF3F because only 8000 and not 8192 bytes are used).

```
FOR I = 53744 TO 65535 : POKE I,0 : NEXT
```

You can do this with a BASIC program, but it takes about 30 seconds to execute. In machine language the whole thing takes place much faster.

Earlier we write a machine language program to display the Commodore 64's character set on the screen. We used an index register to control the program loop. This next loop, requires a range beyond the 256 maximum range of the X and Y index registers. Since you must clear 8000 bytes (length of the bit-mapped area) you can do this with two nested loops. In BASIC it might look like this:

```
100  AD = 57344
110  FOR X = 0 TO 31
120  FOR Y = 0 TO 255
130  POKE AD+Y, 0
140  NEXT Y
150  AD = AD+256
160  NEXT X
```

Here we divided the range of 8192 bytes into 32 parts (or "pages") of 256 bytes each. During each pass through the loop 256 bytes are cleared. Then the base address (AD) is incremented by 256 and the next 256 bytes are cleared. The occurs a total of 32 times, as controlled by the variable X. As an "freebie" we also cleared an extra 192 bytes in the last page (bytes 8001 through 8192). Since these 192 bytes are unused, this won't cause us any problems. Now convert the BASIC program to machine language:

```
100 AD = $E000
110 LDA #0 ; ERASE ACC
120 LDX #0
130 LDY #0
140 STA AD,Y
150 INY
160 BNE SYMB1
170 ; AD = AD + $100
180 INX
190 ; IS X = 31?
200 ; NO, THEN BACK TO LINE 130
210 .EN
```

Some missing pieces from the above program. Can you correctly place the label **SYMB1**? It should be placed at line 140. Variable **AD** is not yet incremented. Use the indirect indexed addressing mode for this. Using this technique, the actual address is obtained from the sum of the two-byte pointer in page zero and the Y-register. Later you can increment this pointer by $100, as called for in line 170. The indexed addressing mode used in line 140 above can access a range of only 256 bytes, but the indirect indexed addressing technique overcomes this limitation. The test of the X-register for 31 in line 190 and the branch back in line 200 are straight-forward. Here's the changes to the above program:

```
100 AD = $E000
110 LDA #0 : ERASE ACC
120 LDX #0
130 SYMB2 LDY #0
140 SYMB1 STA (AD),Y
150 INY
160 BNE SYMB1
170 ; AD = AD + $100
180 INX
190 CPX #32
200 BNE SYMB2
210 .EN
```

Using indirect indexed addressing, address AD must be a two-byte pointer located in page zero, not an absolute address as before. You can use the memory locations $FA and $FB for this pointer. This pointer is loaded with the value $E000 at the beginning of the routine - the low-byte ($00) in $FA and the high-byte ($E0) in $FB. Now add an RTS instruction to the end of the routine, and the final program looks like this:

```
 90 *= $C420
100 LDA #<$E000
102 STA $FA
104 LDA #>$E000
106 STA $FB
110 LDA #0 ; ERASE ACC
120 LDX #31
130 SYMB2 LDY #0
140 SYMB1 STA (AD),Y
150 INY
160 BNE SYMB1
170 INC $FB
180 INX
190 CPX #32
200 BNE SYMB2
205 RTS
210 .EN
```

This routine is assembled beginning at $C420. Save the source program to disk and then assemble it.

```
00FA                 90 AD      =     $FA
00FB                 95 AD1     =     $FB
C420                 97         *=    $C420
C420   A9 00        100         LDA   #<$E000
C422   8D FA 00     102         STA   AD
C425   A9 E0        104         LDA   #>$E000
C427   8D FB 00     106         STA   AD1
C42A   A9 00        110         LDA   #0
C42C   A2 00        120         LDX   #31
C42E   A0 00        130 SYMB2   LDY   #0
C430   91 FA        140 SYMB1   STA   (AD),Y
C432   C8           150         INY
C433   D0 FB        160         BNE   SYMB1
C435   EE FB 00     170         INC   AD1
C438   E8           180         INX
C439   E0 20        190         CPX   #32
C43B   D0 F1        200         BNE   SYMB2
C43D   60           205         RTS
                    210         .EN
```

```
C420 / C43E / 001E
SOURCE FILE IS EXAMPLE 2.SRC
 0  ERRORS

AD      00FA      AD1     00FB      SYMB1  C430      SYMB2  C42E
```

Now that the above program works, can you write a program that presents a more elegant solution? First, you can use zero-page addressing for the two addresses AD and AD1. This is done by using an asterisk before each of the labels. You can also remove the instruction for loading the accumulator with zero in line 110 as this already occurs in line 100; but you must first reverse the order of the assignments in lines 100 to 102 and 104 to 106. If you let the X loop vary from 32 to 0, you can eliminate the comparison in line 190. These improvements enable the program a bit shorter. Here's the new listing:

```
00FA                90 AD      =     $FA
00FB                95 AD1     =     $FB
C420                97         *=    $C420
C420  A9 E0        100         LDA   #>$E000
C422  85 FB        102         STA   *AD1
C424  A9 00        104         LDA   #<$E000
C426  85 FA        106         STA   *AD
C428  A2 20        110         LDX   #32
C42A  A8           120 SYMB2   TAY
C42B  91 FA        130 SYMB1   STA   (AD),Y
C42D  C8           140         INY
C42E  D0 FB        150         BNE   SYMB1
C430  E6 FB        160         INC   *AD1
C432  CA           170         DEX
C433  D0 F5        180         BNE   SYMB2
C435  60           190         RTS
                   200         .EN
```

```
C420 / C436 / 0016
SOURCE FILE IS EXAMPLE 2.SRC
 0  ERRORS
```

```
AD      00FA     AD1     00FB      SYMB1  C42B      SYMB2  C42A
```

With these changes, the program is shorter and faster. Try out the machine language routines by calling them with the following BASIC program:

```
100 SYS 50176 : REM GRAPHICS ON
110 GET A$ : IF A$="" THEN 110
120 SYS 50208 : REM ERASE GRAPHIC IMAGE
130 GET A$ : IF A$="" THEN 130
140 SYS 50192 : REM GRAPHICS OFF
```

After RUNning it, the bit-mapped graphics mode of the Commodore 64 is turned on. When a key is pressed, the graphics screen is cleared. This happens almost immediately. With the earlier BASIC version, this took 30 seconds! By pressing a key again, you turn off the bit-mapped graphics mode and return to normal text mode. Now you can write the corresponding routine to initialize the color memory.

This routine accepts two parameters - one representing the background color and the other the color of the set points. The lower four bits (nybble) of each color memory byte determines the background color and the upper nybble, the color of the set points. Each color memory byte controls a group of 8x8 pixels, as mentioned earlier. For example, if the value of the byte is $10, then the lower nybble is 0 and the upper nybble is 1. This means that the background is black and the foreground is white for that particular 8X8 cell. You can pass the colors to the routine in the accumulator. Try to solve the problem yourself and then compare your solution the one below. Use $C440 as the starting address of the routine. Here's our listing:

```
00FA                90 AD       =     $FA
00FB                95 AD1      =     $FB
C440                97          *=    $C420
C440  A0 C0        100          LDY   #>$C000
C442  84 FB        102          STY   *AD1
C444  A0 00        104          LDY   #<$C000
C446  84 FA        106          STY   *AD
C448  A2 04        110          LDX   #4
C44A  91 FA        130 SYMB1    STA   (AD),Y
C44C  C8           140          INY
C44D  D0 FB        150          BNE   SYMB1
C44F  E6 FB        160          INC   *AD1
C451  CA           170          DEX
C452  D0 F6        180          BNE   SYMB1
C454  60           190          RTS
                   200          .EN

C440 / C455 / 0015
SOURCE FILE IS EXAMPLE 3.SRC
 0  ERRORS

AD      00FA    AD1     00FB      SYMB1  C44A
```

There is a small change to the previous program. The instruction at 180 branches to SYMB1 since the Y-register contains zero; reloading with zero at SYMB2 is superfluous. Try your version now. The starting address is $C440 or 50240. Pass the color value to the accumulator with POKE 780,16

Now that we have taken care of the "housekeeping routines", you can start programming the most important routine for using high resolution graphics: setting and erasing individual points. The next routine demonstrates several programming techniques.

First a word about the layout of the bit-mapped graphics area.

Look at the table on the following page. It illustrates the relationship of the bit-mapped graphics area to the normal 40 column by 25 lines text screen. The numbers in the table represent the offset from the start of the bit-mapped graphics memory that specify if a particular pixel is turned on or off. Let's call the address of the start of the bit-mapped graphics memory + this offset, the **target address.** For example, offset 9 of the bit-mapped graphics area controls the pixel at X=8, Y=1. The target address for this point is $E009 ($E000 + 9), where $E000 is the start of the bit-mapped graphics area.

COLUMN/ LINE	X-coordinate 0-7	8-15	....	312-319	Y-coordinate
	Col 0	Col 1	....	Col 39	
	0	8		312	0
	1	9		313	1
	2	10		314	2
Line 0	3	11	....	315	3
	4	12		316	4
	5	13		317	5
	6	14		318	6
	7	15		319	7
	320	328		632	8
	321	329		633	9
	322	330		634	10
Line 1	323	331	....	635	11
	324	332		636	12
	325	333		637	13
	326	334		638	14
	327	335		639	15
...	....	....	....	....	....
	7680	7688		7992	192
	7681	7689		7993	193
	7682	7690		7994	194
Line 24	7683	7691	....	7995	195
	7684	7692		7996	196
	7685	7693		7997	197
	7686	7694		7998	198
	7687	7695		7999	199

The screen is divided into 25 lines of 40 columns each; each "cell" requires 8 bytes to represent the 64 pixels within that cell (8 pixels per/line X 8 lines/cell). The contents of a single byte controls one row of 8 pixels. Each bit controls an individual pixel on the screen. The highest-order bit represents the pixel on the far left; the lowest-order bit represents the pixel on the far right.

bit number	7	6	5	4	3	2	1	0
contents	1	0	0	0	1	1	0	0

If a byte in the bit-mapped area contains the bit pattern of %10001100 (or $8C in hex), this means that the first, fifth, and sixth pixels from the left are set. Let's call the contents of the byte at the target address the **target value.**

To permit easy manipulation of the graphics, each pixel is addressed by its horizontal (X) and vertical (Y) coordinates. The coordinates range from 0 to 319 for the X-axis (left side of screen to right) and from 0 to 199 for the Y-axis (top of screen to bottom).

First convert the coordinates to actual offsets within the bit-mapped graphics area. Note that each cell is 8-bytes in length. Also note that X-coordinates of 0 thru 7 always fall within the same 8-byte block. The same holds true for X-coordinates of 8 thru 15, 16 thru 23, etc. To convert the X-coordinate value to the start of the appropriate 8-byte block, ignore the lower three bits of the X-coordinate value. Do this by using an AND instruction. To ignore the lower three bits, do the following:

```
X  AND  %1111 1000
```

Here's an example:

```
X-coordinate ==========>            18decimal
Binary representation==>    %0001 0010
Mask for ANDing========>    %1111 1000
                            ---------
Result=================>    %0001 0000   = 16decimal
```

The byte which controls the pixel with an X-coordinate of 18 is in the block beginning at offset 16.

The offset for the X-coordinate is calcuated as follows:

$$OFFSET_X = (XH * 256) + (XL\ AND\ 248)$$

The reason for XL and XH is that an X-coordinate may range from 0 to 319 which is beyond the 255 range of a single byte. Therefore the X-coordinate must be specified using two bytes.

Now for the Y-coordinate. The offset for the Y-coordinate is calculated as follows:

$$OFFSET_Y = (Y\ AND\ 7) + 40 * (Y\ AND\ 248)$$

The complete formula for the calculating the offset for a given X a Y coordinate is as follows:

OFFSET = XH*256 + (XL AND 248) + (Y AND 7) + 40*(Y AND 248)

Now translate the formula into machine language. Use the registers to pass information to the routine as follows:

REGISTER		CONTENTS
Y	=>	Y-coordinate
A	=>	XL-coordinate
X	=>	XH-coordinate

Again, an X-coordinate can range from 0 to 319, so this

requires two bytes of storage. The Y-coordinate is kept in the Y-register. You also need a second 16-bit storage location for storing the offset (SUML/SUMH).

```
100 XL = $FA
110 XH = $FB
120 SUML = $FC
130 SUMH = $FD
140 *= $C460
150 STA *XL
160 STX *XH ; SAVE X-COORDINATE
170 TYA ; Y-COORDINATE
180 AND #$F8
```

First calculate the last term of the formula (EXP1 = 40 * (Y AND 248). The 6510 has no multiplication instruction. Therefore an alternative way of performing multiplication is needed. Recall that a value can be doubled by shifting the contents to the left. Reduce the multiplication by 40 to several doublings:

A * 40 => A * 2 * 2 + A * 2 * 2 * 2

Here, you first get twice the original value (A * 2), then four times (A * 2 * 2), and then five times by adding the original value (A * 2 * 2 + A). Three more doublings by 2 (2 * 2 * 2 = 8) yield the original value times 40.

```
190 STA *$FE ; SAVE ORIGINAL VALUE
200 STA *SUML
210 LDA #0
220 STA *SUMH ; CLEAR HI-BYTE
230 ASL *SUML ; DOUBLING THE ORIGINAL VALUE......
240 ROL *SUMH ; ..IN SUML/SUMH
250 ASL *SUML ; DOUBLING VALUE AGAIN PRODUCES
260 ROL *SUMH ; ..ORIGINAL VALUE * 4 IN SUML/SUMH
```

When shifting 16 bits, you must use a combination of the ASL instruction for the low-byte (8-bits) and the ROL instruction for the high-byte (8-bits). If the ASL instruction causes the highest bit to be shifted out of the operand, the carry flag is set. The ROL instruction shifts takes into account by shifting this carry flag into the low-order bit of the operand, keeping the mathematics exacting. Now you can add the original value.

```
270 CLC ; CLEAR OVERFLOW
280 LDA *SUML
290 ADC *$FE
300 STA *SUML ; STORE RESULT AGAIN
310 LDA *SUMH
320 ADC #0
330 STA *SUMH ;ORIGINAL VALUE * 5 IN SUML/SUMH
```

Why do we add zero to SUMH? If a carry occurs in the SUML addition, it must be taken into account by adding the carry to the high-byte. Adding zero adds any carry which may have been generated by the addition of the low-bytes.

Now we must double the result three more times.

```
340 ASL *SUML
350 ROL *SUMH ; ORIGINAL VALUE * 10 IN SUML/SUMH
360 ASL *SUML
370 ROL *SUMH ; ORIGINAL VALUE * 20 IN SUML/SUMH
380 ASL *SUML
390 ROL *SUMH ; ORIGINAL VALUE * 40 IN SUML/SUMH
```

This takes care care of the first and most difficult term. Now add the second expression (EXP2 = (Y AND 7) + EXP 1).

This is done using another 16-bit addition.

```
400 TYA ; Y-COORDINATE IN ACCUMLATOR
410 AND #7
420 CLC
430 ADC *SUML
440 STA *SUML
450 LDA *SUMH
460 ADC #0
470 STA *SUMH
```

Next, we add the X-value AND 248 (EXP3 = (X AND 248) + EXP2). EXP3 is the offset to the memory location for the specified X and Y coordinates. It is contained in SUML/SUMH after the instruction at line 550 is executed.

```
480 CLC
490 LDA *XL
500 AND #$F8
510 ADC *SUML
520 STA *SUML
530 LDA *XH
540 ADC *SUMH
550 STA *SUMH
```

The bit-mapped graphics begins at $E000, so add this value to the offset (TARGET = $E000 + EXP3) to arrive at the target aaddress.

```
560 CLC
570 LDA #<$E000
580 ASC *SUML
590 STA *SUML
600 LDA #>$E000
610 ADC *SUMH
620 STA *SUMH
```

At last the target address is in SUML/SUMH.

Remember that the contents of the byte at the target address controls 8 pixels on the bit-mapped graphics screen. From the X-coordinate, we must now determine the bit positon within that byte must be set to one in order for the pixel to be turned on.

Earlier we ignored the lowest three bits of the X-coordinate to calculate the target address. Here's where use use the information contained in those three bits. First isolate the lowest three bits of the X-coordinate:

XB = XL AND 7

XB is now a value between 0 and 7 and represents the X-coordinate offset within the bit-mapped control byte. The following table shows the correspondence of the X-coordinate offset and its bit position within the control byte:

X coord. offset		bit position
0	=>	7
1	=>	6
2	=>	5
3	=>	4
4	=>	3
5	=>	2
6	=>	1
7	=>	0

The lowest three bits of the X-coordinate and the bit positon are inverses of each other. You can convert an X-coordinate offset to a bit position by using the exclusive

OR instruction:

```
630 LDA *XL ;low-byte of X-coordinate
640 AND #7  ;isolate the lowest three bits
650 EOR #7  ;convert to bit position
```

From the earlier calculations, we found the target address. From the above calculations, we found the bit position which needs to be set at that target address to turn on the pixel. We know that each bit position has a certain value, which we call the target value. Now we have to convert that bit position to the target value. This target value is then stored at the target address to set the specific pixel.

To calculate the target value corresponding to this bit position we shift a **one** bit to the left for the number of times indicated by the bit position. Here's the code:

```
660 TAX ; bit position in X-register
670 LDA #1 ;"one" bit
680 SHIFT DEX
690 BMI OK
700 ASL A ; shift to left
710 BNE SHIFT
720 OK ...
```

The bit position is contained in the accumulator after executing the instruction in line 650. The target value is calculated by shifting left as many times as specified by the X-register. In lines 680 and 690 the contents of the X-register are decremented and checked to see if it's negative (less than zero). If not, continue shifting another position to the left. The branch in line 710 is always executed because the result of the shift is never equal to zero.

Storing the target value contained in the accumulator at the target address turns on the desired pixel.

But there's another consideration. Remember that each target address controls 8 pixels. If another pixel is already set at that target address, then storing the above target value destroys the previous value and erase the other pixels controlled by the same target address.

To avoid this, you should combine the previous value at the target address with new target value. Use the OR instruction for this. By ORing the old value with the new target value, any previously set pixels are not erased.

The target address is pointed to by the contents of SUML/SUMH. To combine the previous value with the new value, you can do the following:

```
720 OK LDY #0
730 ORA (SUML),Y
740 STA (SUML),Y
750 RTS
```

Now the new pixel is set and we are done. There is one small point which we overlooked.

The OR instruction in line 730 accesses the contents of a memory location in the range from $E000 to $FFFF. The Commodore 64 normally returns the value of the contents of the kernal ROM also located at these same addresses (but in a different bank). A "switch" controls access to either the ROM or RAM at those addresses. The ORA (SUML),Y instruction above would access the ROM and not the bit-mapped graphics area. To access the RAM containing the bit-mapped graphics area, set the switch (I/O register) located at address 1. When you do this, you must inhibit the interrupts because the interrupt routines are not available while the ROM is switched off. After the contents at the target address are updated, the interrupts are re-enabled.

```
730 LDX #$34 ; RAM CONFIGURATION
740 SEI ; INHIBIT INTERRUPTS
750 STX *1
760 ORA (SUML),Y
770 STA (SUML),Y ; SET POINT
780 LDX #$37 ; ROM CONFIGURATION
790 STX *1
800 CLI ; ENABLE INTERRUPTS
810 RTS
820 .EN
```

Here is the complete assembly listing of all of the routines that we've talked about in this chapter:

```
00FA                100 XL      =     $FA
00FB                110 XH      =     $FB
00FC                120 SUML    =     $FC
00FD                130 SUMH    =     $FD
C460                140         *=    $C460
C460  85 FA         150         STA   *XL
C462  86 FB         160         STX   *XH ; SAVE X-COORDINATE
```

```
C464  98         170           TYA           ; Y-COORDINATE
C465  29 F8      180           AND   #$F8
C467  85 FE      190           STA   *$FE
C469  85 FC      200           STA   *SUML
C46B  A9 00      210           LDA   #0
C46D  85 FD      220           STA   *SUMH
C46F  06 FC      230           ASL   *SUML
C471  26 FD      240           ROL   *SUMH
C473  06 FC      250           ASL   *SUML
C475  26 FD      260           ROL   *SUMH
C477  18         270           CLC             ; ERASE CARRY
C478  A5 FC      280           LDA   *SUML
C47A  65 FE      290           ADC   *$FE
C47C  85 FC      300           STA   *SUML
C47E  A5 FD      310           LDA   *SUMH
C480  69 00      320           ADC   #0
C482  85 FD      330           STA   *SUMH
C484  06 FC      340           ASL   *SUML
C486  26 FD      350           ROL   *SUMH
C488  06 FC      360           ASL   *SUML
C48A  26 FD      370           ROL   *SUMH
C48C  06 FC      380           ASL   *SUML
C48E  26 FD      390           ROL   *SUMH
C490  98         400           TYA              ; Y-COORDINATE
C491  29 07      410           AND   #7
C493  18         420           CLC
C494  65 FC      430           ADC   *SUML
C496  85 FC      440           STA   *SUML
C498  A5 FD      450           LDA   *SUMH
C49A  69 00      460           ADC   #0
C49C  85 FD      470           STA   *SUMH
C49E  18         480           CLC
C49F  A5 FA      490           LDA   *XL
C4A1  29 F8      500           AND   #$F8
C4A3  65 FC      510           ADC   *SUML
C4A5  85 FC      520           STA   *SUML
C4A7  A5 FB      530           LDA   *XH
C4A9  65 FD      540           ADC   *SUMH
C4AB  85 FD      550           STA   *SUMH
C4AD  18         560           CLC
C4AE  A9 00      570           LDA   #<$E000
C4B0  65 FC      580           ADC   *SUML
C4B2  85 FC      590           STA   *SUML
C4B4  A9 E0      600           LDA   #>$E000
C4B6  65 FD      610           ADC   *SUMH
C4B8  85 FD      620           STA   *SUMH
C4BA  A5 FA      630           LDA   *XL
C4BC  29 07      640           AND   #7
C4BE  49 07      650           EOR   #7
C4C0  AA         660           TAX
C4C1  A9 01      670           LDA   #1
C4C3  CA         680 SHIFT     DEX
C4C4  30 03      690           BMI   OK
C4C6  0A         700           ASL   A
C4C7  D0 FA      710           BNE   SHIFT
```

```
C4C9   A0 00          720 OK      LDY    #0
C4CB   A2 34          730         LDX    #$34
C4CD   78             740         SEI    *1
C4CE   86 01          750         STX
C4D0   11 FC          760         ORA    (SUML),Y
C4D2   91 FC          770         STA    (SUML),Y
C4D4   A2 37          780         LDX    #$37
C4D6   86 01          790         STX    *1
C4D8   58             800         CLI
C4D9   60             810         RTS
                      820         .EN

C460 / C4DA / 007A
SOURCE FILE IS EXAMPLE 3.SRC
 0   ERRORS

OK      C4C9     SHIFT  C4C3      SUMH    00FD       SUML    00FC
XH      00FB     XL     00FA
```

Now to try out these routines, we can type this short BASIC program to call the high resolution graphics:

```
100 SYS 50176 : REM GRAPHICS ON
110 SYS 50208 : REM ERASE GRAPHIC IMAGE
120 POKE 780,16 : REM BLACK/WHITE
130 SYS 50240 : REM INITIALIZE COLOR
140 FOR X=0 TO 319
150 POKE 780,X AND 255 : REM X-LO
160 POKE 781,X / 256   : REM X-HI
170 POKE 782,X * 0.625 : REM Y
180 SYS 50272 : SET POINT
190 NEXT
200 GET A$ : IF A$="" THEN 200
210 SYS 50192 : REM TURN OFF
```

RUNning this program draws a diagonal line from the upper left to the lower right corner. Pressing a key returns the Commodore 64 to the normal text mode.

Now consider how a point can be erased. The routine to calculate the target address is the same for setting or for erasing a point. By changing line 760, you can cause the routine to erase a pixel instead of setting it. Look at what happens when you set a point with ORA.

```
previous bit pattern   % 01001000
pattern for new pixel  % 00010000
                       ----------
result of ORA          % 01011000
```

The new point is set by using an ORA instruction. To erase the same point use the AND instruction.

```
previous bit pattern             % 01011000
pattern for pixel to be erased   % 00010000
                                 ----------
result of AND                    % 00010000
```

Something is wrong here! All the points are erased except for the one you want to erase. The bit values must be inverted prior to ANDing. You can can do this with the EOR intruction.

```
pixel to be erased      % 00010000
invert all bits         % 11111111
                        ----------
gives the new pattern   % 11101111
```

Except for the point to be erased, all the bits are now set and the AND operation with the original value works.

```
previous bit pattern   % 01011000
new pattern            % 11101111
                       ----------
correct pattern        % 01001000
```

Now add the erase function to the other routines. You can use the carry flag to signal whether the point is to be set or erased. If the carry flag is clear, then the routine erases the pixel. The routine must make note of the condition of the carry flag. Use the PHP instruction to save the status register on the stack, as in line 145. Examine the flags by using a PLP instruction in line 735. Here are the remaining changes to the program:

```
760 BCC ERASE
770 ORA (SUML),Y
780 BCS OK2
790 ERASE EOR #$FF ; INVERT
800 AND (SUML),Y
810 OK2 STA (SUML)
820 LDX #$37
830 STX *1
840 CLI
850 RTS
860 .EN
```

If the carry flag is clear, jump to line 790 where the bits are inverted with EOR #$FF. The AND instruction is executed and the result is stored. If, on the other hand, the carry flag is set, then the bit is set with ORA as before and the new value is again stored at the target address. The complete listing is shown below:

```
00FA              100 XL     =     $FA
00FB              110 XH     =     $FB
00FC              120 SUML   =     $FC
00FD              130 SUMH   =     $FD
C460              140        *=    $C460
C460              145        PHP
C461   85 FA      150        STA   *XL
C463   86 FB      160        STX   *XH ; X-COORDINATE
C465   98         170        TYA       ; Y-COORDINATE
```

```
C466  29 F8     180          AND  #$F8
C468  85 FE     190          STA  *$FE
C46A  85 FC     200          STA  *SUML
C46C  A9 00     210          LDA  #0
C46E  85 FD     220          STA  *SUMH
C470  06 FC     230          ASL  *SUML
C472  26 FD     240          ROL  *SUMH
C474  06 FC     250          ASL  *SUML
C476  26 FD     260          ROL  *SUMH
C478  18        270          CLC            ; ERASE CARRY
C479  A5 FC     280          LDA  *SUML
C47B  65 FE     290          ADC  *$FE
C47D  85 FD     300          STA  *SUML
C47F  A5 FD     310          LDA  *SUMH
C481  69 00     320          ADC  #0
C483  85 FD     330          STA  *SUMH
C485  06 FC     340          ASL  *SUML
C487  26 FD     350          ROL  *SUMH
C489  06 FC     360          ASL  *SUML
C48B  26 FD     370          ROL  *SUMH
C48D  06 FC     380          ASL  *SUML
C48F  26 FD     390          ROL  *SUMH
C491  98        400          TYA            ; Y-COORDINATE
C492  29 07     410          AND  #7
C494  18        420          CLC
C495  65 FC     430          ADC  *SUML
C497  85 FC     440          STA  *SUML
C499  A5 FD     450          LDA  *SUMH
C49B  69 00     460          ADC  #0
C49D  85 FD     470          STA  *SUMH
C49F  18        480          CLC
C4A0  A5 FA     490          LDA  *XL
C4A2  29 F8     500          AND  #$F8
C4A4  65 FC     510          ADC  *SUML
C4A6  85 FC     520          STA  *SUML
C4A8  A5 FB     530          LDA  *XH
C4AA  65 FD     540          ADC  *SUMH
C4AC  85 FD     550          STA  *SUMH
C4AE  18        560          CLC
C4AF  A9 00     570          LDA  #<$E000
C4B1  65 FC     580          ADC  *SUML
C4B3  85 FC     590          STA  *SUML
C4B5  A9 E0     600          LDA  #>$E000
C4B7  65 FD     610          ADC  *SUMH
C4B9  85 FD     620          STA  *SUMH
C4BB  A5 FA     630          LDA  *XL
C4BD  29 07     640          AND  #7
C4BF  49 07     650          EOR  #7
C4C1  AA        660          TAX
C4C2  A9 01     670          LDA  #1
C4C4  CA        680 SHIFT    DEX
C4C5  30 03     690          BMI  OK
C4C7  0A        700          ASL  A
C4C8  D0 FA     710          BNE  SHIFT
C4CA  A0 00     720 OK       LDY  #0
```

```
C4CC  A2 34        730          LDX   #$34
C4CE  28           735          PLP
C4CF  78           740          SEI
C4D0  86 01        750          STX   *1
C4D2  90 04        760          BCC   ERASE
C4D4  11 FC        770          ORA   (SUML),Y
C4D6  B0 04        780          BCS   OK2
C4D8  49 FF        790 ERASE    EOR   #$FF
C4DA  31 FC        800          AND   (SUML),Y
C4DC  91 FC        810 OK2      STA   (SUML),Y
C4DE  A2 37        820          LDX   #$37
C4E0  86 01        830          STX   *1
C4E2  58           840          CLI
C4E3  60           850          RTS
                   860          .EN
C460 / C4E4 / 0084
SOURCE FILE IS EXAMPLE 4.SRC
 0  ERRORS

ERASE  C4D8    OK    C4CA    OK2   C4DC    SHIFT  C4C4
SUMH   00FD    SUML  00FC    XH    00FB    XL     00FA
```

Now change the previous BASIC "test" program:

```
100 SYS 50176 : REM GRAPHICS ON
110 SYS 51208 : REM ERASE GRAPHIC IMAGE
120 POKE 780,16
130 SYS 50240 : REM SET COLOR
140 I=1
150 FOR X=0 TO 319
160 POKE 780, X AND 255 : REM X LO
170 POKE 781, X AND 255 : REM X HI
180 POKE 782, X * 0.625 : REM Y
190 POKE 783, I : REM SET/ERASE
200 SYS 50272 : NEXT
210 GET A$ : IF A$="" THEN I=1-I : GOTO 150
220 SYS 50192 : REM GRAPHICS OFF
```

This program draws a diagonal line across the screen and then erases it again. The routine determines if a pixel is to be set or erased, by the condition of the carry flag which is passed in memory location 783. Because the carry flag occupies bit position zero within the status register, the corresponding values are one and zero.

You can stop the program by pressing a key. The original screen contents is preserved, just as the graphics screen is also preserved. When you want to switch back to high resolution graphics mode, simply call the routine to erase the screen and you can start anew. Now you can experiment some more with the routine for the color representation.

```
100 SYS 50176 : REM GRAPHICS ON
110 SYS 51208 : REM ERASE GRAPHICS
120 POKE 780,16
130 SYS 50240 : REM SET COLOR
140 REM
150 FOR X=70 TO 150 : FOR Y=X TO 199
160 POKE 780, X : REM X LO
170 POKE 781, 0 : REM X HI
180 POKE 782, Y : REM Y
190 POKE 783, 1 : REM SET
200 SYS 50272 : NEXT : NEXT
210 FOR C=0 TO 255
220 FOR I=1 TO 500 : NEXT
230 POKE 780, C
240 SYS 50240 : REM COLOR
250 NEXT
260 SYS 50192 : REM GRAPHICS OFF
```

This program draws a figure and then displays it in all of the 256 possible color combinations.

To summarize, you have learned about indirect indexed addressing; you have worked with the logical operations to set and erase designated bits; you have also used the stack for storing data; and you have performed 16-bit additions and shifts.

An important programming concept still missing is the use of subroutines. This is discussed in the next section.

8. Extending BASIC

In the previous section we passed parameters to the graphics routine by means of POKE commands. Now we present a more elegant way of doing this.

This technique passes parameters the same way as parameters are passs to the BASIC commands.

Let's take a simple BASIC command:

```
POKE A, B
```

The variables A and B are arguments for the POKE command. The rules of BASIC allow you to use any expressions, constants or subscripted variables in place of A and B. For example, the following is a legal BASIC statement:

```
POKE A(1000)/750*INT(X%/9),EXP(ABS(SIN(3*A)))+2
```

The BASIC interpreter uses a routine in its ROMs to evaluate the value of the expressions. You can let the BASIC interpreter do hard evaluation work by calling this routine from your own programs. In addition, you can perform range checking by using various entry points to the BASIC ROM routines.

When evaulating the arguments for the POKE routine, for

example, the routines check to make sure that the first parameter is a value between 0 and 65535 (16-bit). If not, the error message **ILLEGAL QUANTITY** is issued. The routines then check the second parameter for a value between 0 to 255, and the same error message is given if it fails this test.

How can you use these routines in your own programs?

First you must understand a programming technique that we have not discussed up to this point - the subroutine.

You have probably used subroutines when programming in BASIC. The corresponding commands in BASIC are:

GOSUB and RETURN

The GOSUB command branches to a given line. It differs from the GOTO instruction in that the interpreter remembers the place from which it branched. When the subroutine is finished, and the interpreter encounters a RETURN, the previously saved return address is fetched and execution branches back to the place from where the subroutine call was made.

The 6510 microprocessor has two instructions for managing of subroutines. These commands correspond exactly to their BASIC counterparts.

JSR and RTS

JSR (jump to subroutine) calls the subroutine while the RTS instruction (return from subroutine) takes care of branching back to the calling routine. When do you use these instructions?

Subroutines in machine language programs are used in the same circumstances as in BASIC. If a certain routine is to be used more than once, it should be made into a subroutine.

What does the processor do when it encounters a JSR instruction?

Before it branches to the subroutine, it saves the current address of the program counter so that it knows where to return after the subroutine is complete. Where does it save this information? It uses the stack!

A subroutine call saves the current address (two bytes) of the program counter on the stack. Later, when the RTS instruction is encountered, the address on the stack replaces the program counter contents. The instruction following the JSR is then executed.

So that the 6510 knows at which place on the stack to save to and retrieve from, there is a register called the stack pointer (shortened to SP). This register is a pointer to the current position of the stack. Let's see what happens when the JSR and RTS commands are executed.

```
C000  20 00 C1  JSR $C100
C003  ....

C100  60        RTS
```

When this program is started at address $C000, a call is made to the subroutine at address $C100. In our example, the RTS instruction is encountered immediately and the processor returns to the instruction following the subroutine call, which is $C003 in our case. Let's see what happens to the stack and the stack pointer.

Address	Instruction	Stack pointer	Stack	
$C000	JSR $C100	$F9	$01F9	XX

The data from any previous operations is located at stack address $01F9. When the processor encounters the JSR instruction, it takes the contents of the program counter, increments it by two and divides it into low and high bytes. It takes the high-byte and stores it at the address to which the stack pointer points. The stack pointer is then decremented by one:

Address	Instruction	Stack pointer	Stack	
$C000	JSR $C000	$F8	$01F9	C0
			$01F8	XX

Now the low-byte of the address is saved on the stack and

the stack pointer is again decremented. The program counter is then set to the starting address of the subroutine:

```
Address   Instruction   Stack pointer     Stack
 $C100      RTS              $F7        $01F9  C0
                                        $01F8  02
                                        $01F7  XX
```

So during a JSR, the program counter is saved on the stack and the stack pointer is decremented by two. The stack pointer always points to the next free location on the stack.

The RTS instruction performs these functions in reverse. First the stack pointer is incremented and then the low-byte is fetched from the stack:

```
Address   Instruction   Stack pointer     Stack
 $C100      RTS              $F8        $01F9  C0
                                        $01F8  02
                                        $01F7  XX
```

The value $02 is placed into the low-byte of the program counter. Then stack pointer is incremented:

```
Address   Instruction   Stack pointer     Stack
 $C100      RTS              $F9        $01F9  C0
                                        $01F8  02
                                        $01F7  XX
```

$C0 is pulled from the stack and becomes the high-byte of the program counter. The program counter now contains $C002.

The program counter is incremented by one and the next instruction is fetched from $C003:

```
Address    Instruction Stack pointer    Stack
 $C003       ...             $F9      $01F9  C0
                                      $01F8  02
                                      $01F7  XX
```

Notice that the stack pointer contains the same value after the return from the subroutine as before the call.

It is also possible to nest subroutines with this technique. If a subroutine is called from another subroutines, its return address is saved on the stack. The stack pointer is set to $F5 in our example. The last return address is fetched by the next RTS instruction and the stack pointer is incremented to $F7. RTS will always jumps back to the address of the last subroutine call. Through this, it is possible to nest levels of subroutines.

The 6510 microprocessor can save and retrieve the contents of the accumulator and the processor stack register to and from the stack. The commands are PHA and PLA for the accumulator and PHP and PLP for the status register. These commands also affect the stack pointer. Using these instructions you can, for example, save the contents of the status register and later retrieve it. Thus the stack can be used as a "scratchpad".

```
PHA  ; accumulator to stack
TYA
PHA  ; and Y register
TXA
PHA  ; and X register
...
PLA
TAX  ; get X register back
PLA
TAY  ; and Y register
PLA  ; and accumulator
```

The X and Y registers cannot be saved directly onto the stack. You have to transfer the contents of the the X-register or Y-register to the accumulator first and then placed the contents to the stack with a PHA instruction. Notice that the registers must be pulled from the stack in the reverse order they were pushed on. This is in accordance with to the principle of the stack. The last value place on the stack is the first value retrieved from the stack - in a last in-first out (LIFO) order.

The operation of the stack and the stack pointer can be illustrated by the single-step simulator. After each step, you can observe the contents of the registers. The simulator becomes a very useful learning tool.

Now let's can return to our discussions about the BASIC interpreter routines for passing parameters.

A routine called **GETBYT** in the BASIC ROMs, reads an expression from BASIC text, checks it for a range from 0 and 255, and returns this value in the X-register.

Another routine called **FRMNUM**, converts a expression to 16-bit (0 to 65535) values.

The routine **GETADR**, checks an expression for a range from 0 to 65535. If it is valid, the low-byte of the value is returned in memory location $14 and the high-byte of the value is returned in memory location $15. The addresses of these routines are listed below.

Earlier we talked about how the BASIC interpreter reads each line character by character in order to find the BASIC keywords. In doing so, BASIC keeps track of its place in the line by using an internal variable called **TXTPTR** (for text pointer). At any given time, TXTPTR points to the BASIC text which the interpreter is processing.

If you want to pass a parameter from a BASIC program to a machine language routine, you can use the BASIC command:

SYS AAAAA,PPP

AAAAA is the decimal address of the machine language routine. PPP is the parameter that you are passing to the machine langauge routine.

If you want to pass several parameters, you must separate these parameters from each other with commas. The BASIC interpreter has a routine to check for commas This routine is called **CHKCOM** and checks to see if TXTPTR is pointing to a comma.

If you want to read a character directly from the BASIC text, the routine **CHRGOT** gets the character pointed to by TXTPTR and puts it into the accumulator. The routine **CHRGET** does the same thing but first increments TXTPTR before getting the character.

These routines also set certain flags which give additional information about the character read. If the zero flag is set, then either a zero byte (end-of-line in BASIC programs) or a colon ":" was read, indicating the end of the statement. If a digit is read, the carry flag is clear.

Here is a summary of the addresses:

```
GETBYT    $B79E
FRMNUM    $AD8A
GETADR    $B7F7
CHKCOM    $AEFD
CHRGOT    $0079
CHRGET    $0073
GETPAR    $B7EB
```

To get a 16-bit parameter followed by an 8-bit parameter such as for the POKE command, you can use the routine GETPAR. The routine **GETPAR** calls the following routines in order: FRMNUM, GETADR, CHKCOM, and GETBYT.

You can use GETPAR for the bit-mapped graphics routines

because the value for the X-coordinate is a 16-bit number (0-319) and the value for the Y-coordinate (0-199) is an 8-bit number. If the values exceed 65535 or 255, respectively, the BASIC interpreter responds with **ILLEGAL QUANTITY.** So GETPAR checks the ranges of the coordinates and display this error message if required.

To use these routines for parameter passing, a call would look like this:

SYS 50240,X,Y

When BASIC encounters this statement, it sets up to execute the machine language routine beginning at memory location 50240. The BASIC TXTPTR is left pointing at the first comma following the 50240.

Using this technique, you do not have to POKE the parameters into memory. The program is also a lot easier to follow.

Now let's reprogram the graphics routines again, but incoprorating the new techniques:

```
100 JSR CHKCOM ; COMMA FOLLOWING?
110 JSR GETPAR ; GET COORDINATES
120 STX YCOOR  ; SAVE Y-COORDINATE
130 LDA $14
140 STA XL ; X-COORDINATE LO
150 LDA $15
160 STA XH
```

First we check for a comma which separates the SYS address from the X-coordinate. Next we use the routine which gets two parameters, GETPAR. The value of the one-byte parameter, the Y-coordinate, is returned in the X-register which we save at the address YCOOR. The value of the second parameter, the X-coordinate returned in $14/$15 and saved in XL and XH. Now check that the X and Y-coordinates lie in the permitted value range. If the Y-coordinate is less than 200, it is legal, otherwise display **ILLEGAL QUANTITY.** The same type of range checking is performed for the X-coordinate.

```
170 CPX #200 ; Y >= 200?
180 BCC OK
190 ERROR JMP ILLEGAL
200 OK LDA XH
210 CMP #>320
220 BCC OK1
230 BNE ERROR
235 LDA XL
240 CMP #<320
250 BCS ERROR
260 OK1 ...
```

The remainder of the program is the same as the earlier version.

9. Input/Output Operations

In BASIC you use specific commands to input characters from the keyboard, display them on the screen and communicate with peripherals. Some of the BASIC commands to do this are:

```
OPEN
CMD
PRINT#
INPUT#
CLOSE
```

In machine language programming you use similar techniques. The operating system already contains routines which correspond to the BASIC commands above. You can use these routines to perform input or output operations.

Some of the routines follows:

OPEN

This routine requires three parameters: the logical file number, the device address, and the secondary address, and an optional filename. These parameters are set by the routines SETFLS and SETNAM. The OPEN routine itself needs no parameters but it does require a prior calls to the other routines.

SETFLS

To use **SETLFS,** load the accumulator with the logical filenumber, the X-register with the device number, and the Y-register with the secondary address and then call this routine to set these parameters for the OPEN routine.

SETNAM

This routine is defines a filename. Load the accumulator with the of the filename (0 indicates that no filename will be used); place the address of the filename (the first memory location it is stored in) in the X-registser (low-byte) and Y-register (high-byte).

PRINT

Load the accumulator with the character you wish to output and then call this routine. Normally the output goes to the screen. If you want to output to the printer, for example, you must first open a file to the printer (device 4) with the OPEN routine and then call the next routine.

CHKOUT

This routine corresponds to the CMD instruction in BASIC. To output a character to an opened file, load the X-register with the logical file number and call the subroutine CHKOUT. All output from the PRINT instruction is sent to this device until cancelled with the next routine.

CLRCH

CLRCH cancels the CMD mode set by the CHKOUT instruction. It requires no parameters.

INPUT

This routine gets a character from the keyboard and returns it in the accumulator. To read data from a file, first open and then activate it with the next routine.

CHKIN

Load the logical file number in the X-register and call this routine. After calling this routine, all input is read from this device until cancelled with CLRCH.

CLOSE

Load the logical file number into the accumulator and call this routine to close a file.

The following table contains the addresses of these routines.

Routine	Address
OPEN	$FFC0
SETFLS	$FFBA
SETNAM	$FFBD
PRINT	$FFD2
CHKOUT	$FFC9
CLRCH	$FFCC
INPUT	$FFCF
CHKIN	$FFC6
CLOSE	$FFC3

To demonstrate how to use these routines, let's convert the following BASIC commands to machine language:

```
OPEN 1,8,15
PRINT# 1,"I"
CLOSE 1
```

```
100 LDA #1 ; LOGICAL FILE NUMBER
110 LDX #8 ; DEVICE NUMBER
120 LDY #15 ; SECONDARY ADDRESS
130 JSR SETFLS
140 LDA #0
150 JSR SETNAM ; NO NAME
160 JSR OPEN ; OPEN FILE
170 LDX #1 ; LOGICAL FILE NUMBER
180 JSR CHKOUT ; OUTPUT TO FILE
190 LDA #73 ; "I"
200 JSR PRINT
210 JSR CLRCH
220 LDA #1 ; LOGICAL FILE NUMBER
230 JSR CLOSE
240 RTS
```

Lines 100 to 130 setup the parameters for the OPEN. There is no filename, so the length of the filename is set to zero in line 140 to 150. Line 160 OPENs the file. Now output to the logical file 1 is enabled (lines 170-180) and the ASCII value of "I" is transmitted to the disk (device 8) by the PRINT routine to initialize the diskette. Routine CLRCH, redirects output to the screen. Finally, lines 220 and 230 CLOSEs the file and execution returns to BASIC (or other calling program) with the RTS.

The next example, reads the error channel of the disk drive and display the error message on the screen. You can do this in BASIC like this:

```
100 OPEN 1,8,15
110 INPUT#1, A,B$,C,D
120 PRINT A; B$; C; D
130 CLOSE 1
```

Because we can output the error message directly to the screen, we need no variables in our program. We simply read characters from the channel until the status variable ST, is equal to 64, signaling the end of the error message. We can do this with the following BASIC program:

```
100 OPEN 1,8,15
110 GET#1, A$ : PRINT A$;
120 IF ST <> 64 THEN 110
130 CLOSE 1
```

To do this in machine language, you must know that the

status variable of the operating system ST, is stored in location 144 or $90. Let's try the machine language version:

```
 10 OPEN   = $FFC0
 20 SETFLS = $FFBA
 30 SETNAM = $FFBD
 40 PRINT  = $FFD2
 50 CLRCH  = $FFCC
 60 INPUT  = $FFCF
 70 CHKIN  = $FFC6
 80 CLOSE  = $FFC3
 90 STATUS = $90 ; STATUS VARIABLE
100 LDA #1 ; LOGICAL FILE NUMBER
110 LDX #8 ; DEVICE NUMBER
120 LDY #15 ; SECONDARY ADDRESS
130 JSR SETFLS
140 LDA #0
150 JSR SETNAM ; NO NAME
160 JSR OPEN ; OPEN FILE
170 LDX #1 ; LOGICAL FILE NUMBER
180 JSR CHKIN ; INPUT FROM ERROR CHANNEL
190 L1 JSR INPUT ; GET CHARACTER
200 JSR PRINT ; AND OUTPUT
210 BIT STATUS ; TEST STATUS
220 BVC L1
230 JSR CLRCH ; INPUT FROM DEFAULT
240 LDA #1
250 JSR CLOSE
260 RTS
270 .EN
```

The routine from the previous program for OPENing the file is the same. This time, we input data from the file. Lines 170 and 180 setup to do this. The X-register is loaded with the logical file number 1 and the routine CHKIN is called. Input is now read from the disk drive. Line 190 reads a character from the disk and line 200 writes it to the screen with JSR PRINT. The output goes to the screen because we did not previously use CHKOUT. The status variable ST is tested with the BIT instruction. If the end of the file is reached, status variable ST is set to 64. 64 is equal to 2^6 or

%01000000 in binary. Therefore bit 6 of this memory location is set at end of file. What does the BIT instruction do? It copies bit 6 of the addressed memory location into the V flag and bit 7 into the N flag. After the BIT instruction, you need only test to see if the V flag is set. The instruction BVC branches if the V flag is clear. In this case, the end has not been reached and we branch back to the read more from the disk. If the V flag is set, we reset the input channel with JSR CLRCH and close the file.

Assemble this program and try it out. Remember, however, that our assembler allows a maximum of only five characters for symbol names.

```
C000                OPEN    =      $FFC0
C000                SETFLS  =      $FFBA
C000                SETNAM  =      $FFBD
C000                PRINT   =      $FFD2
C000                CLRCH   =      $FFCC
C000                INPUT   =      $FFCF
C000                CHKIN   =      $FFC6
C000                CLOSE   =      $FFC3
C000                STATUS  =      $90
C000 A9 01                  LDA    #1       ;LOGICAL FILE NUMBER
C002 A2 08                  LDX    #8       ;DEVICE NUMBER
C004 A0 0F                  LDY    #15      ;SECONDARY ADDRESS
C006 20 BA FF               JSR    SETFLS
C009 A9 00                  LDA    #0       ;NO FILENAME
C00B 20 BD FF               JSR    SETNAM
C00E 20 C0 FF               JSR    OPEN     ;OPEN FILE
C011 A2 01                  LDX    #1       ;INPUT
C013 20 C6 FF               JSR    CHKIN    ;FROM ERROR CHANNEL
C016 20 CF FF  L1           JSR    INPUT    ;CHARACTER FROM DISK
C019 20 D2 FF               JSR    PRINT    ;AND OUTPUT
C01C 24 90                  BIT    STATUS   ;TEST STATUS
C01E 50 F6                  BVC    L1
C020 20 CC FF               JSR    CLRCH
C023 A9 01                  LDA    #1
C025 20 C3 FF               JSR    CLOSE    ;CLOSE FILE
C028 60                     RTS
```

Now you can try out the machine language routine by typing:

SYS 49152

The error message from the disk appears on the screen, such as:

```
00, OK,00,00
```

10. A BASIC Loader Program

You can enter the machine language program as a sequence of numbers in DATA statements. They can be READ by a BASIC program and stored in memory with POKE. You can output the values in decimal by means of a small BASIC program and insert these as DATA statements in a loader program. Here is a program written in BASIC, which does this automatically.

It is used as follows. First load your machine language program. Then type in the following BASIC program and RUN it. You are now asked to enter the starting and ending addresses of the machine language program. The program creates a complete loader program on the printer with an automatically generated checksum. The checksum is simply the sum of all the values. The values are summed while being loaded and the checksum contained within the program is checked against the value generated by the program. If the two values aren't equal, an appropriate message is displayed.

By doing this you can determine if the user made an error while typing in the data.

```
100 OPEN 1,4 : Z = 100
110 INPUT "START ADDRESS ";A
120 INPUT "END ADDRESS   ";E
130 CMD1 : PRINT Z "FOR I =" A "TO" E
140 I=A : Z=Z+10 : PRINT Z "READ X : POKE I,X : S=S+X : NEXT"
150 Z=Z+10 : N=0 : PRINT Z "DATA ";
```

```
160 X=PEEK(I) : S=S+X : PRINT RIGHT$("  "+STR$(X),3);:N=N+1
170 IF I=E THEN PRINT : GOTO200
180 I=I+1:IF N=12 THEN PRINT:GOTO150
190 PRINT ",";:GOTO160
200 PRINT Z+10 "IF S<>" S "THEN PRINT" CHR$(34) "ERROR
    IN DATA !!" CHR$(34) :  PRINT " : END" : END
210 PRINT Z+20 "PRINT " CHR$(34) "OK" CHR$(34)
220 PRINT#1:CLOSE1
```

11. 6510 Disassembler

This section contains a program called a disassembler. The purpose of a disassembler is to translate machine language programs in memory back to the mnemonics used for entering assembly language programs. From the sequence $A9, $80, for example, the disassembler generates LDA #$80. The disassembler is simply started with RUN and it asks for the starting and ending addresses of the memory range to disassemble. The output then appears on the screen, but it can be redirected to the printer with an appropriate OPEN instruction and CMD assignment.

Here's a brief description of the operation of the disassembler. The program gets a byte from memory and interprets it as an operation code. This op code serves as an index in a table of instruction mnemonics, instruction lengths and addressing modes. The disassembler knows the form of the operand and where the next instruction begins from these tables.

The disassembler can be used for your own machine language programs as well as for the disassembly of the operating system and BASIC interpreter. You can often find hints and tips for your own programs there. Better yet is the commented listing of operating system which you can find in The Anatomy of the Commodore 64.

Here is the disassembler listing.

```
100 REM 6510 DISASSEMBLER
110 DIMMN$(255),AD(255),H$(15)
120 FF=255:HI=256:UL=2↑16:SC=2↑15-1
130 PRINT"{CLR}{C/DN}{C/DN}{C/DN}{C/RT}{C/RT}{C/RT}{C/RT}{C/RT}{C/RT}
{C/RT}{C/RT}{C/RT}{C/RT}{C/RT}6510 DISASSEMBLER"
140 FORI=0TO15:READH$(I):NEXT
150 FORI=0TO255:READMN$(I),AD(I):NEXT
160 PRINT"{C/DN}START ADDRESS:-    $****{C/LF}{C/LF}{C/LF}{C/LF}{C/LF}
170 GOSUB540:S=A
180 PRINT"{C/DN}END ADDRESS  :-    $****{C/LF}{C/LF}{C/LF}{C/LF}{C/LF}
{C/LF}";:INPUTA$:PRINT

190 GOSUB540:E=A
200 FORP=STOE
210 A=P:GOSUB450:REM ADDRESS
220 PRINT" ";:A=PEEK(P):GOSUB480:PRINT" ";:I=PEEK(P):OP=AD(I)
230 ONOPGOSUB510,520,520,510,530,520,520,530,530,520,520,520,530
240 PRINT" ";MN$(I)" ";
250 ONOPGOSUB270,280,290,300,310,320,330,340,350,360,370,380,400
260 NEXTP:GOTO160
270 PRINT:RETURN
280 PRINT"#";:GOSUB490:P=P+1:PRINT:RETURN
290 GOSUB490:P=P+1:PRINT:RETURN
300 PRINT" A":RETURN
310 GOSUB420:P=P+2:PRINT:RETURN
320 GOSUB490:P=P+1:PRINT",X":RETURN
330 GOSUB490:P=P+1:PRINT",Y":RETURN
340 GOSUB420:P=P+2:PRINT",X":RETURN
350 GOSUB420:P=P+2:PRINT",Y":RETURN
360 PRINT"(";:GOSUB490:P=P+1:PRINT"),Y":RETURN
370 PRINT"(";:GOSUB490:P=P+1:PRINT",X)":RETURN
380 T=PEEK(P+1):Q=T+HI*(T>127)+2+P
390 A=INT(Q/HI)*HI+((Q+(Q>SC)*UL)ANDFF):PRINT"$";:GOSUB450:P=P+1:
400 PRINT"(";:GOSUB420
410 PRINT")":P=P+2:RETURN
420 PRINT"$";
430 A=PEEK(P+1)+HI*PEEK(P+2)
440 REM HEX ADDRESS A
450 HB=INT(A/HI):A=A-HI*HB
460 PRINTH$(HB/16)H$(HBAND15);
470 REM HEX BYTE A
480 PRINTH$(A/16)H$(AAND15);:RETURN
490 PRINT"$";
500 A=PEEK(P+1):GOTO480
510 PRINT"      ";:RETURN
520 GOSUB500:PRINT"   ";:RETURN
530 GOSUB500:PRINT" ";:A=PEEK(P+2):GOTO480
540 IFASC(A$)=42THENEND
550 A=0:FORI=1TO4:V=ASC(RIGHT$(A$,I))-48:V=V+(V>9)*7:A=A+V*(16↑
(I-1)):NEXT:RETURN
1000 DATA 0,1,2,3,4,5,6,7,8,9,A,B,C,D,E,F
1010 DATA"BRK",1,"ORA",11,"???",1
1020 DATA"???",1,"???",1,"ORA",3
1030 DATA"ASL",3,"???",1,"PHP",1
1040 DATA"ORA",2,"ASL",4,"???",1
1050 DATA"???",1,"ORA",5,"ASL",5
```

```
1060 DATA"???",1,"BPL",12,"ORA",10
1070 DATA"???",1,"???",1,"???",1
1080 DATA"ORA",6,"ASL",6,"???",1
1090 DATA"CLC",1,"ORA",9,"???",1
1100 DATA"???",1,"???",1,"ORA",8
1110 DATA"ASL",8,"???",1,"JSR",5
1120 DATA"AND",11,"???",1,"???",1
1130 DATA"BIT",3,"AND",3,"ROL",3
1140 DATA"???",1,"PLP",1,"AND",2
1150 DATA"ROL",4,"???",1,"BIT",5
1160 DATA"AND",5,"ROL",5,"???",1
1170 DATA"BMI",12,"AND",10,"???",1
1180 DATA"???",1,"???",1,"AND",6
1190 DATA"ROL",6,"???",1,"SEC",1
1200 DATA"AND",9,"???",1,"???",1
1210 DATA"???",1,"AND",8,"ROL",8
1220 DATA"???",1,"RTI",1,"EOR",11
1230 DATA"???",1,"???",1,"???",1
1240 DATA"EOR",3,"LSR",3,"???",1
1250 DATA"PHA",1,"EOR",2,"LSR",4
1260 DATA"???",1,"JMP",5,"EOR",5
1270 DATA"LSR",5,"???",1,"BVC",12
1280 DATA"EOR",10,"???",1,"???",1
1290 DATA"???",1,"EOR",6,"LSR",6
1300 DATA"???",1,"CLI",1,"EOR",9
1310 DATA"???",1,"???",1,"???",1
1320 DATA"EOR",8,"LSR",8,"???",1
1330 DATA"RTS",1,"ADC",11,"???",1
1340 DATA"???",1,"???",1,"ADC",3
1350 DATA"ROR",3,"???",1,"PLA",1
1360 DATA"ADC",2,"ROR",4,"???",1
1370 DATA"JMP",13,"ADC",5,"ROR",5
1380 DATA"???",1,"BVS",12,"ADC",10
1390 DATA"???",1,"???",1,"???",1
1400 DATA"ADC",6,"ROR",6,"???",1
1410 DATA"SEI",1,"ADC",9,"???",1
1420 DATA"???",1,"???",1,"ADC",8
1430 DATA"ROR",8,"???",1,"???",1
1440 DATA"STA",11,"???",1,"???",1
1450 DATA"STY",3,"STA",3,"STX",3
1460 DATA"???",1,"DEY",1,"???",1
1470 DATA"TXA",1,"???",1,"STY",5
1480 DATA"STA",5,"STX",5,"???",1
1490 DATA"BCC",12,"STA",10,"???",1
1500 DATA"???",1,"STY",6,"STA",6
1510 DATA"STX",7,"???",1,"TYA",1
1520 DATA"STA",9,"TXS",1,"???",1
1530 DATA"???",1,"STA",8,"???",1
1540 DATA"???",1,"LDY",2,"LDA",11
1550 DATA"LDX",2,"???",1,"LDY",3
1560 DATA"LDA",3,"LDX",3,"???",1
1570 DATA"TAY",1,"LDA",2,"TAX",1
1580 DATA"???",1,"LDY",5,"LDA",5
1590 DATA"LDX",5,"???",1,"BCS",12
1600 DATA"LDA",10,"???",1,"???",1
1610 DATA"LDY",6,"LDA",6,"LDX",7
1620 DATA"???",1,"CLV",1,"LDA",9
1630 DATA"TSX",1,"???",1,"LDY",8
```

```
1640 DATA"LDA",8,"LDX",9,"???",1
1650 DATA"CPY",2,"CMP",11,"???",1
1660 DATA"???",1,"CPY",3,"CMP",3
1670 DATA"DEC",3,"???",1,"INY",1
1680 DATA"CMP",2,"DEX",1,"???",1
1690 DATA"CPY",5,"CMP",5,"DEC",5
1700 DATA"???",1,"BNE",12,"CMP",10
1710 DATA"???",1,"???",1,"???",1
1720 DATA"CMP",6,"DEC",6,"???",1
1730 DATA"CLD",1,"CMP",9,"???",1
1740 DATA"???",1,"???",1,"CMP",8
1750 DATA"DEC",8,"???",1,"CPX",2
1760 DATA"SBC",11,"???",1,"???",1
1770 DATA"CPX",3,"SBC",3,"INC",3
1780 DATA"???",1,"INX",1,"SBC",2
1790 DATA"NOP",1,"???",1,"CPX",5
1800 DATA"SBC",5,"INC",5,"???",1
1810 DATA"BEQ",12,"SBC",10,"???",1
1820 DATA"???",1,"???",1,"SBC",6
1830 DATA"INC",6,"???",1,"SED",1
1840 DATA"SBC",9,"???",1,"???",1
1850 DATA"???",1,"SBC",8,"INC",8
1860 DATA"???",1
```

Program Description

100 - 150	Initialization; build tables
160 - 190	Prompt for starting and ending addresses for the disassembly and conversion to decimal.
200 - 260	FOR-NEXT loop for disassembly from starting to ending address. Line 220 gets the instruction code and the current address is output. Line 230 outputs the operands depending on the address mode. Line 240 outputs the instruction mnemonic. Line 250 displays the operand corresponding to the addressing mode. Line 260 ends the loop and jumps back to the input.
280 - 410	Output the operand as the address mode dictates.
420 - 530	Output hexadecimal forms of bytes and addresses.
540 - 550	Conversion of a hex number to decimal.
1000 - 1860	Tables containing the instruction mnemonics and addressing modes.

Variable	Description
MN$(255)	Table of instruction words
AD(255)	Table of address modes
H$(15)	Field with hex digits
FF	constant 255
HI	constant 256
UL	constant 65536
SC	constant 32767
A$	string variable for hex number
S	start address
E	end address
P	program counter
OP	addressing mode

12. Using a Machine Language Monitor

Here's another tool to aid in machine language development. The tool is called a monitor.

A monitor can be used to enter machine language programs. You can displays and changes the contents of memory locations and the registers. Additionally, you can save and load machine language programs to tape or diskette. You can execute machine language programs from it. If you end such a program with a BRK instruction, control is returned to the monitor and the contents of the registers are be displayed.

The following is an explaination of the commands available with the SUPERMON monitor. SUPERMON is a public domain monitor written by well know Commodore expert Jim Butterfield who has given us so many useful tools. SUPERMON is available free of charge from many sources including most local user groups. We have explained the use of SUPERMON beacuse it is so widely available.

SUPERMON is started by LOAD "SUPERMON",8 and activated with RUN. The monitor responds with:

```
..JIM BUTTERFIELD
B*
    PC    SR AC XR YR SP
.; 9835   31 40 E6 00 F6
```

B indicates that the monitor was entered by "BRK".

The labels are as follows:

```
PC  program counter
SR  status register
AC  accumulator
XR  x-register
YR  y-register
SP  stack pointer
```

The contents of those registers appear below the labels. You can change the contents of any register by moving the cursor over the old contents, overwriting it with the new value, and pressing the <RETURN> key. If you want to change the flags, the status register must be changed.

SUPERMON uses the period . as its prompt. When you see the period on the screen, SUPERMON is asking you to enter a command.

You can display the register contents at any time by entering R at the prompt:

```
.R
```

and pressing the <RETURN> key. The contents of the registers is displayed, just as above.

The next command displays and allows you to change the contents of memory. At the prompt, enter M followed by the first and last address you wish to see. The starting and ending addresses are entered as four-digit hexadecimal numbers such as:

```
.M A0A0 A0AF
.: A0A0  C4 46 4F D2 4E 45 58 D4
.: A0A8  44 41 54 C1 49 4E 50 55
```

SUPERMON displays the contents memory below your entry. You can interpret the output in the following way:

An address is displayed after the colon. This is the address of the first of eight following bytes. In this example, address $A0A0 contains the value $C4. Address $A0A1 contains $46, and so on. A total of eight bytes are displayed per line. SUPERMON displays as many lines as specified by the address range which you entered.

To change a single byte in memory, move the cursor over the old value, type in the new value, and press the <RETURN> key.

If you want to execute a program, use the instruction G. If the program starts at address $CF20, enter

```
.G CF20
```

This begins the execution of a machine language program beginning at the specified address. First, however, the registers are be loaded with the values displayed with the R command. The last instruction in the machine language program should be BRK which causes execution to return to the monitor when the program is done. When a BRK is executed, the register contents are then automatically displayed, as below:

```
B*
     PC   SR AC XR YR SP
.; CF39  B3 8F 73 B0 F6
```

The B indicates that your program ended with a BRK instruction and that the monitor was entered by means of this BRK instruction. The program counter points to the byte immediately after the BRK instruction. If you have several BRK commands in your program, this information tells you at which point your program was stopped.

Knowing this, you can develop the following method for testing and debugging programs. Place BRK instructions at all of the important locations in the program so that the program stops at these points. Then check the register contents and data in memory. If the program has run properly up to this point, replace the BRK instruction with the original instruction and place a BRK instruction at the next critical location. This way you can test your program step by step until it runs to your satisfaction.

Loading and saving programs is accomplished through the use of the L and S commands. The following syntax is used:

```
.L "NAME",XX
```

To load a program type the name of the program in quotation marks followed by a comma separating it the device address given as a two-digit hex number area . If you want to load the program GRAPHIC from disk, for example, the instruction would look like this:

```
.L "GRAPHIC",08
```

If you want to load from cassette, you use the device address 01.

```
.L "GRAPHICS",01
```

The SAVE command works the same way. Because the computer must know the memory range to save, it is necessary to give a starting and an ending address. The ending address must be one greater than the last byte you want to save. The command looks like this:

```
.S "PROGRAM",08,7000,8000
```

It writes the memory range from $7000 to $7FFF to the disk under the name "PROGRAM". Here too the device address 01 can be entered in order to save to the cassette drive.

Another function of SUPERMON is the built-in disassembler. By entering D followed by an address range you can display machine language programs on the screen in disassembled format. The format is the same as that used by the disassembler written earlier in BASIC. If you enter the following instruction:

```
.D B824 B82C
```

the following is displayed:

```
., B824   20 EB B7   JSR $B7EB
., B827   8A         TXA
., B828   A0 00      LDY #$00
., B82A   91 14      STA ($14),Y
., B82C   60         RTS
```

We disassembled a part of the BASIC interpreter which performs the POKE command.

Another useful command in SUPERMON allows one area of memory to be copied to another. Enter the starting and ending addresses of the area to be copied and the starting address of the destination area. The contents of the original area are left unchanged.

```
.T 6000 6FFF 3000
```

copies the area from $6000 to $6FFF to the addresses from $3000 to $3FFF.

Another useful function hunt command. With this command you can search for specific values in memory. The results displayed are the addresses at which those values are found.

```
.H E000 EFFF 20 D2 FF
```

searches through the memory range from $E000 to $EFFF for the values $20, $D2, $FF. This command will display a list of addresses at which these values were found. In this example we would see:

```
E10C
```

SUPERMON found the values 20 D2 FF at the area of memory starting at E10C.

Another command fills memory with a particular value. With this you can fill a range of memory with constant values.

```
.F 8000 8FFF 00
```

fills the area from $8000 to $8FFF with zero bytes.

You can use the next command to assemble single lines of machine language. By entering the following:

```
.A 0800 LDA #$FF
```

SUPERMON will assemble the machine language codes A9 FF into memory beginning at $0800. This function makes it easy to enter short machine language program.

The last command exits from SUPERMON and returns you to the BASIC interpreter. Simply enter:

```
.X
```

and the interpreter will respond with READY. If you later wish to use the monitor again, you can return to it by entering

```
SYS 49152
```

APPENDIX A -

Addressing Modes and Operation Codes

MNEMONIC	ADDRESSING MODE								
*	A	#	ZP	AB	ABX	ABY	ZPX	ZPY	,X)	),Y
ADC	-	69	65	6D	7D	79	75	-	61	71
AND	-	29	25	2D	3D	39	35	-	21	31
ASL	0A	-	06	0E	1E	-	16	-	-	-
BIT	-	-	24	2C	-	-	-	-	-	-
CMP	-	C9	C5	CD	DD	D9	D5	-	C1	D1
CPX	-	E0	E4	EC	-	-	-	-	-	-
CPY	-	C0	C4	CC	-	-	-	-	-	-
DEC	-	-	C6	CE	DD	-	D6	-	-	-
EOR	-	49	45	4D	5D	59	55	-	41	51
INC	-	-	E6	EE	FD	-	F6	-	-	-
LDA	-	A9	A5	AD	BD	B9	B5	-	A1	B1
LDX	-	A2	A6	AE	-	BE	-	B6	-	-
LDY	-	A0	A4	AC	BC	-	B4	-	-	-
LSR	4A	-	46	4E	5E	-	56	-	-	-
ORA	-	09	05	0D	1D	19	15	-	01	11
ROL	2A	-	26	2E	3E	-	36	-	-	-
ROR	6A	-	66	6E	7E	-	76	-	-	-
SBC	-	E9	E5	ED	FD	F9	F5	-	E1	F1
STA	-	-	85	8D	9D	99	95	-	81	91
STX	-	-	86	8E	-	-	-	96	-	-
STY	-	-	84	8C	-	-	94	-	-	-

APPENDIX B

Grouped Instructions

Branch Instr.	BPL	BMI	BVC	BVS	BCC	BCS	BNE	BEQ
	10	30	50	70	90	B0	D0	F0
Transfer Instr.	TXA	TAX	TYA	TAY	TSX	TXS		
	8A	AA	98	A8	BA	9A		
Stack Instr.	PHP	PLP	PHA	PLA				
	08	28	48	68				
Jump Instr.	BRK	JSR	RTI	RTS	JMP	JMP	NOP	
	00	20	40	60	4C	6C	EA	
Flag Instr.	CLC	SEC	CLI	SEI	CLV	CLD	SED	
	18	38	58	78	B8	D8	F8	
Inc/Dec Instr.	DEY	INY	DEX	INX				
	88	C8	CA	E8				

APPENDIX C

Conversion Table   Decimal - Hexadecimal - Binary

Decimal	Hex	Binary	Decimal	Hex	Binary
0	00	00000000	49	31	00110001
1	01	00000001	50	32	00110010
2	02	00000010	51	33	00110011
3	03	00000011	52	34	00110100
4	04	00000100	53	35	00110101
5	05	00000101	54	36	00110110
6	06	00000110	55	37	00110111
7	07	00000111	56	38	00111000
8	08	00001000	57	39	00111001
9	09	00001001	58	3A	00111010
10	0A	00001010	59	3B	00111011
11	0B	00001011	60	3C	00111100
12	0C	00001100	61	3D	00111101
13	0D	00001101	62	3E	00111110
14	0E	00001110	63	3F	00111111
15	0F	00001111	64	40	01000000
16	10	00010000	65	41	01000001
17	11	00010001	66	42	01000010
18	12	00010010	67	43	01000011
19	13	00010011	68	44	01000100
20	14	00010100	69	45	01000101
21	15	00010101	70	46	01000110
22	16	00010110	71	47	01000111
23	17	00010111	72	48	01001000
24	18	00011000	73	49	01001001
25	19	00011001	74	4A	01001010
26	1A	00011010	75	4B	01001011
27	1B	00011011	76	4C	01001100
28	1C	00011100	77	4D	01001101
29	1D	00011101	78	4E	01001110
30	1E	00011110	79	4F	01001111
31	1F	00011111	80	50	01010000
32	20	00100000	81	51	01010001
33	21	00100001	82	52	01010010
34	22	00100010	83	53	01010011
35	23	00100011	84	54	01010100
36	24	00100100	85	55	01010101
37	25	00100101	86	56	01010110
38	26	00100110	87	57	01010111
39	27	00100111	88	58	01011000
40	28	00101000	89	59	01011001
41	29	00101001	90	5A	01011010
42	2A	00101010	91	5B	01011011
43	2B	00101011	92	5C	01011100
44	2C	00101100	93	5D	01011101
45	2D	00101101	94	5E	01011110
46	2E	00101110	95	5F	01011111
47	2F	00101111	96	60	01100000
48	30	00110000	97	61	01100001
			98	62	01100010

Decimal	Hex	Binary	Decimal	Hex	Binary
99	63	01100011	148	94	10010100
100	64	01100100	149	95	10010101
101	65	01100101	150	96	10010110
102	66	01100110	151	97	10010111
103	67	01100111	152	98	10011000
104	68	01101000	153	99	10011001
105	69	01101001	154	9A	10011010
106	6A	01101010	155	9B	10011011
107	6B	01101011	156	9C	10011100
108	6C	01101100	157	9D	10011101
109	6D	01101101	158	9E	10011110
110	6E	01101110	159	9F	10011111
111	6F	01101111	160	A0	10100000
112	70	01110000	161	A1	10100001
113	71	01110001	162	A2	10100010
114	72	01110010	163	A3	10100011
115	73	01110011	164	A4	10100100
116	74	01110100	165	A5	10100101
117	75	01110101	166	A6	10100110
118	76	01110110	167	A7	10100111
119	77	01110111	168	A8	10101000
120	78	01111000	169	A9	10101001
121	79	01111001	170	AA	10101010
122	7A	01111010	171	AB	10101011
123	7B	01111011	172	AC	10101100
124	7C	01111100	173	AD	10101101
125	7D	01111101	174	AE	10101110
126	7E	01111110	175	AF	10101111
127	7F	01111111	176	B0	10110000
128	80	10000000	177	B1	10110001
129	81	10000001	178	B2	10110010
130	82	10000010	179	B3	10110011
131	83	10000011	180	B4	10110100
132	84	10000100	181	B5	10110101
133	85	10000101	182	B6	10110110
134	86	10000110	183	B7	10110111
135	87	10000111	184	B8	10111000
136	88	10001000	185	B9	10111001
137	89	10001001	186	BA	10111010
138	8A	10001010	187	BB	10111011
139	8B	10001011	188	BC	10111100
140	8C	10001100	189	BD	10111101
141	8D	10001101	190	BE	10111110
142	8E	10001110	191	BF	10111111
143	8F	10001111	192	C0	11000000
144	90	10010000	193	C1	11000001
145	91	10010001	194	C2	11000010
146	92	10010010	195	C3	11000011
147	93	10010011	196	C4	11000100

Decimal	Hex	Binary	Decimal	Hex	Binary
197	C5	11000101	227	E3	11100011
198	C6	11000110	228	E4	11100100
199	C7	11000111	229	E5	11100101
200	C8	11001000	230	E6	11100110
201	C9	11001001	231	E7	11100111
202	CA	11001010	232	E8	11101000
203	CB	11001011	233	E9	11101001
204	CC	11001100	234	EA	11101010
205	CD	11001101	235	EB	11101011
206	CE	11001110	236	EC	11101100
207	CF	11001111	237	ED	11101101
208	D0	11010000	238	EE	11101110
209	D1	11010001	239	EF	11101111
210	D2	11010010	240	F0	11110000
211	D3	11010011	241	F1	11110001
212	D4	11010100	242	F2	11110010
213	D5	11010101	243	F3	11110011
214	D6	11010110	244	F4	11110100
215	D7	11010111	245	F5	11110101
216	D8	11011000	246	F6	11110110
217	D9	11011001	247	F7	11110111
218	DA	11011010	248	F8	11111000
219	DB	11011011	249	F9	11111001
220	DC	11011100	250	FA	11111010
221	DD	11011101	251	FB	11111011
222	DE	11011110	252	FC	11111100
223	DF	11011111	253	FD	11111101
224	E0	11100000	254	FE	11111110
225	E1	11100001	255	FF	11111111
226	E2	11100010			

APPENDIX D

APPENDIX D
Table of 6510 Instruction Codes

	0	1	2	4	5	6	8	9	A	C	D	E
0	BRK	ORA ,X)			ORA ZP	ASL ZP	PHP	ORA #	ASL A		ORA AB	ASL AB
1	BPL	ORA),Y			ORA ZPX	ASL ZPX	CLC	ORA ABY			ORA ABX	ASL ABX
2	JSR	AND ,X)		BIT ZP	AND ZP	ROL ZP	PLP	AND #	ROL A	BIT AB	AND AB	ROL AB
3	BMI	AND),Y			AND ZPX	ROL ZPX	SEC	AND ABY			AND ABX	ROL ABX
4	RTI	EOR ,X)			EOR ZP	LSR ZP	PHA	EOR #	LSR A	JMP AB	EOR AB	LSR AB
5	BVC	EOR),Y			EOR ZPX	LSR ZPX	CLI	EOR ABY			EOR ABX	LSR ABX
6	RTS	ADC ,X)			ADC ZP	ROR ZP	PLA	ADC #	ROR A	JMP IND	ADC AB	ROR AB
7	BVS	ADC),Y			ADC ZPX	ROR ZPX	SEI	ADC ABY			ADC ABX	ROR ABX
8		STA ,X)		STY ZP	STA ZP	STX ZP	DEY		TXA	STY AB	STA AB	STX AB
9	BCC	STA),Y		STY ZPX	STA ZPX	STX ZPY	TYA	STA ABY	TXS		STA ABX	
A	LDY #	LDA ,X)	LDX #	LDY ZP	LDA ZP	LDX ZP	TAY	LDA #	TAX	LDY AB	LDA AB	LDX AB
B	BCS	LDA),Y		LDY ZPX	LDA ZPX	LDX ZPY	CLV	LDA ABY	TSX	LDY ABX	LDA ABX	LDX ABY
C	CPY #	CMP ,X)		CPY ZP	CMP ZP	DEC ZP	INY	CMP #	DEX	CPY AB	CMP AB	DEC AB
D	BNE	CMP),Y			CMP ZPX	DEC ZPX	CLD	CMP ABY			CMP ABX	DEC ABX
E	CPX #	SBC ,X)		CPX ZP	SBC ZP	INC ZP	INX	SBC #	NOP	CPX AB	SBC AB	INC AB
F	BEQ	SBC),Y			SBC ZPX	INC ZPX	SED	SBC ABY			SBC ABX	INC ABX

The operation codes can be determined from the table as follows:

The left-most column gives the high nybble of the opcode while the top line gives the low nybble of the opcode. Example: EOR # has the operation code $49.

The abbreviations for the addressing mode have the following meanings:

Abbreviation	Addressing Mode	Instruction Length
A	accumulator	1
AB	absolute	3
ABX	absolute, Y indexed	3
ABY	absolute, X indexed	3
IND	indirect	3
ZP	zero page	2
ZPX	zero page, X indexed	2
ZPY	zero page, Y indexed	2
#	immediate	2
,X)	X indexed, indirect	2
),Y	indirect, Y indexed	2

APPENDIX E

OPERATION CODES AND FLAG SETTINGS

*	Bit map	N	V	B	D	I	Z	C
ADC	011XXX01	X	X				X	X
AND	001XXX01	X					X	
ASL	000XXX10	X					X	X
BCC	10010000							
BCS	10110000							
BEQ	11110000							
BIT	0010X100	M	M				X	
BMI	00110000							
BNE	10010000							
BPL	00010000							
BRK	00000000			1		1		
BVC	01010000							
BVS	01110000							
CLC	00011000							0
CLD	11011000				0			
CLI	01011000					0		
CLV	10111000		0					
CMP	110XXX01	X					X	X
CPX	1110XX00	X					X	X
CPY	1100XX00	X					X	X
DEC	110XX110	X					X	
DEX	11001010	X					X	
DEY	10001000	X					X	
EOR	010XXX01	X					X	
INC	000XX110	X					X	
INX	11101000	X					X	
INY	11001000	X					X	
JMP	01X01100							
JSR	00100000							
LDA	101XXX01	X					X	
LDX	101XXX10	X					X	
LDY	101XXX00	0					X	X
NOP	11101010							
ORA	000XXX01	X					X	

*	Bit map	N	V	B	D	I	Z	C
PHA	01001000							
PHP	00001000							
PLA	01101000	X					X	
PLP	00101000	X	X	X	X	X	X	X
ROL	001XXX10	X					X	X
ROR	011XXX10	X					X	X
RTI	01000000	X	X	X	X	X	X	X
RTS	01100000							
SBC	111XXX01	X	X				X	X
SEC	00111000							1
SED	11111000				1			
SEI	01111000					1		
STA	100XXX01							
STX	100XX110							
STY	100XX100							
TAX	10101010	X					X	
TAY	10101000	X					X	
TSX	10111010	X					X	
TXA	10001010	X					X	
TXS	10011010							
TYA	10011000	X					X	

If the bit map of a instruction contains one or more Xs, these bits are dependent on the address mode. An X in a flag column indicates that that flag is affected by the instruction. A 0 or 1 means that the flag is cleared or set, respectively. If no entry is given under a particular flag, the instruction in question does not affect that flag.

APPENDIX F

OPTIONAL DISKETTE ORDERING INFORMATION

The listings in this book for the LEA Assembler, 6510 Single-Step Simulator, Disassembler and SUPERMON monitor are available on a ready to run 1541 Format Diskette.

By purchasing this diskette, you can eliminate typing these programs into your Commodore 64 from the listings.

The programs on the diskette have been fully tested and are available for $14.95 + $2.00 ($5.00 foreign) postage and handling charge.

To order, send name, address and a check, money order or credit card information to:

ABACUS SOFTWARE
P.O. BOX 7211
GRAND RAPIDS, MI 49510

For fast service, order by phone - 616 / 241-5510.

Be sure to ask for the "Optional Diskette for the Machine Language Book for the Commodore 64"

FOR COMMODORE-64 HACKERS ONLY!

The ultimate source for Commodore-64 Computer information

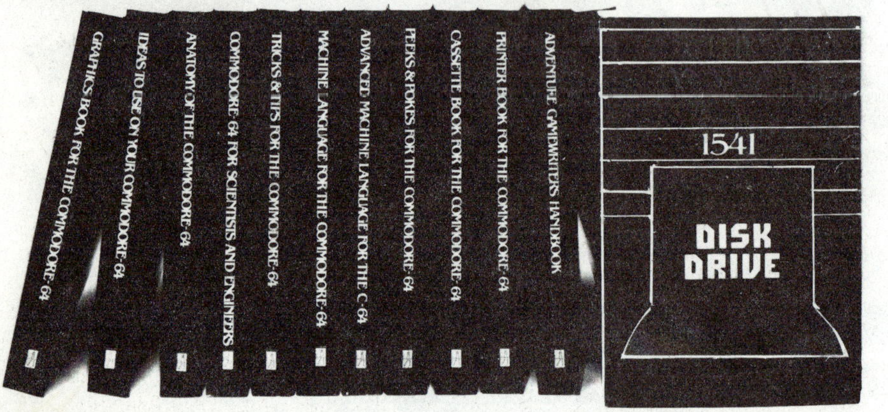

OTHER BOOKS AVAILABLE SOON

THE ANATOMY OF THE C-64

is the insider's guide to the lesser known features of the Commodore 64. Includes chapters on graphics, sound synthesis, input/output control, sample programs using the kernal routines, more. For those who need to know, it includes the complete disassembled and documented ROM listings.

ISBN-0-916439-00-3 300pp $19.95

THE ANATOMY OF THE 1541 DISK DRIVE

unravels the mysteries of using the misunderstood disk drive. Details the use of program, sequential, relative and direct access files. Include many sample programs - FILE PROTECT, DIRECTORY, DISK MONITOR, BACKUP, MERGE, COPY, others. Describes internals of DOS with completely disaddembled and commented listings of the 1541 ROMS.

ISBN-0-916439-01-1 320pp $19.95

MACHINE LANGUAGE FOR C-64

is aimed at those who want to progress beyond BASIC. Write faster, more memory efficient programs in machine language. Test is specifically geared to Commodore 64. Learns all 6510 instructions. Includes listings for 3 full length programs: ASSEMBLER, DISASSEMBLER and amazing 6510 SIMULATOR so you can "see" the operation of the '64.

ISBN-0-916439-02-X 200pp $14.95

TRICKS & TIPS FOR THE C-64

is a collection of easy-to-use programming techniques for the '64. A perfect companion for those who have run up against those hard to solve programming problems. Covers advanced graphics, easy data input, BASIC enhancements, CP/M cartridge on the '64, POKEs, user defined character sets, joystick/mouse simulation, transferring data between comuters, more. A treasure chest.

ISBN-0-916439-03-8 250pp $19.95

GRAPHICS BOOK FOR THE C-64

takes you from the fundamentals of graphic to advanced topics such as computer aided design. Shows you how to program new character sets, move sprites, draw in HIRES and MULTICOLOR, use a lightpen, handle IRQs, do 3D graphics, projections, curves and animation. Includes dozens of samples.

ISBN-0-916439-05-4 280pp $19.95

ADVANCED MACHINE LANGUAGE FOR THE C-64

gives you an intensive treatment of the powerful '64 features. Author Lothar Englisch delves into areas such as interrupts, the video controller, the timer, the real time clock, parallel and serial I/O, extending BASIC and tips and tricks from machine language, more.

ISBN-0-916439-06-2 200pp $14.95

IDEAS FOR USE ON YOUR C-64

is for those who wonder what you can do with your '64. It is written for the novice and presents dozens of program listing the many, many uses for your computer. Themes include: auto expenses, electronic calculator, recipe file, stock lists, construction cost estimator, personal health record diet planner, store window advertising, computer poetry, party invitations and more.

ISBN-0-916439-07-0 200pp $12.95

PRINTER BOOK FOR THE C-64

finally simplifies your understanding of the 1525, MPS/801, 1520, 1526 and Epson compatible printers. Packed with examples and utility programs, you'll learn how to make hardcopy of text and graphics, use secondary addresses, plot in 3-D, and much more. Includes commented listing of MPS 801 ROMs.

ISBN-0-916439-08-9 350pp. $19.95

SCIENCE/ENGINEERING ON THE C-64

is an introduction to the world of computers in science. Describes variable types, computational accuracy, various sort alogrithms. Topics include linear and nonlinear regression, CHI-square distribution, Fourier analysis, matrix calculations, more. Programs from chemistry, physics, biology, astronomy and electronics. Includes many program listings.

ISBN-0-916439-09-7 250pp $19.95

CASSETTE BOOK FOR THE C-64

(or Vic 20) contains all the information you need to know about using and programming the Commodore Datasette. Includes many example programs. Also contains a new operating system for fast loading, saving and finding of files.

ISBN-0-916439-04-6 180pp. $12.95

DEALER INQUIRIES ARE INVITED

IN CANADA CONTACT:
The Book Centre, 1140 Beaulac Street
Montreal, Quebec H4R1R8 Phone: (514) 322-4154

AVAILABLE AT COMPUTER STORES, OR WRITE:

Abacus Software
P.O. BOX 7211 GRAND RAPIDS, MI 49510
Exclusive U.S. DATA BECKER Publishers

For postage & handling, add $4.00 (U.S. and Canada), add $6.00 for foreign. Make payment in U.S. dollars by check, money order of charge card. (Michigan Residents add 4% sales tax.)

VISA MasterCard

FOR QUICK SERVICE PHONE (616) 241-5510

Commodore 64 is a reg. T.M. of Commodore Business Machines